SYSTEMATIC
SELF-OBSERVATION

Dear Doug
Your work has been
a valuable resource !
With aloha,
Noelie & Alan

NOELIE RODRIGUEZ
ALAN RYAVE

Qualitative Research Methods
Volume 49

Sage Publications
International Educational and Professional Publisher
Thousand Oaks   London   New Delhi

For Chin Hwei, Sara Sen-Mei, and Chris, Nina, Emma, Ronnie, Peg, Albert, Dr. Lee, Barbara, Nancy, Richard, Diana, Steve, Marilyn, Diane, Hal, Trina, Ellen, Kristina, Jim, Ted, Lee, Scott, Ferd, Don, Luika, Roselyn, Vivian, Iva, Bob, Rago, Fred, John, Anson, Janina, Barry, Wade, Lou, Majid, Seatree, Julie, Ah Quon, Selene, Pat, Gerdine, Stephanie, Mike, Bert, and all the Yuens.

For information:

Sage Publications, Inc.
2455 Teller Road
Thousand Oaks, California 91320
E-mail: order@sagepub.com

Sage Publications Ltd.
6 Bonhill Street
London EC2A 4PU
United Kingdom

Sage Publications India Pvt. Ltd.
M-32 Market
Greater Kailash I
New Delhi 110 048 India

Printed in the United States of America

Library of Congress Cataloging-in-Publication Data

Rodriguez, Noelie.
    Systematic self-observation / Noelie Rodriguez, Alan Ryave.
        p. cm. — (Qualitative research methods; v. 49)
    Includes bibliographical references.
    ISBN 0-7619-2307-1 (cloth: alk. paper)
    ISBN 0-7619-2308-X (pbk.: alk paper)
    1. Observation (Psychology) 2. Introspection. 3.
Psychology—Research—Methodology. I. Ryave, Alan. II. Title. III.
Series.
    BF76.6.O27 R63 2001
    300'.7'2—dc21
                                    2001004187

01 02 03 04 05 06 10 9 8 7 6 5 4 3 2 1

Acquiring Editor:	Heidi Van Middlesworth
Production Editor:	Denise Santoyo
Typesetter:	Denyse Dunn
Copyeditor:	Elisabeth Magnus

CONTENTS

ACKNOWLEDGMENTS

The authors want to take this opportunity to thank *all* of their teachers at the University of California, Los Angeles, with special thanks to Harvey Sacks, John Horton, and Warren Ten Houten. Our work is inspired by many, but we especially appreciate the vision of Harvey Sacks, Erving Goffman, Harold Garfinkel, George Psathas, Steve Riskin, Emanuel Schegloff, Howard Schwartz, Marilyn Garber, Martin Karasch, and John Heritage. We also appreciate the patience and support of our dear family, friends, and colleagues.

SERIES EDITORS' INTRODUCTION

The reflective and reflexive nature of observational data is hardly a matter of debate. From William James to Erving Goffman, students of the social world have struggled with the problematic character of personal observation while nonetheless relying on personal observation—their own as well as others'—as the source of empirical and theoretical findings and generalizations. While all analysts recognize that what we see, what we say, and what we do are in large measure sociologically and culturally constrained if not precisely rule governed, such constraints and rules are typically examined at some remove, through reports on and from others, and as applicable more to those who are studied than those who are doing the studying. They are thus treated as part of the habituated but distinct form of life under the research gaze. Rarely are such constraints and rules seen as universal building blocks of social life itself, as practices in which we all engage and, when viewed broadly, make social life possible—here, there, and everywhere.

Noelie Rodriguez and Alan Ryave begin their treatment of Systematic Self-Observation in Volume 49 of the Sage Series on Qualitative Research Methods by calling on the universality of self-consciousness. They rightly note that much of the most fascinating social data are in fact personal in nature and observational in character. Moreover, such data are easily located in those mundane, unremarkable reflections and exchanges that form the thought processes and conversational rituals of our everyday lives. If, for example, social relations are generated (or terminated), smoothed (or disrupted), or tightened (or loosened) through the telling of lies, the withholding of compliments, or the keeping of secrets, what better observers exist than the tellers of lies, the withholders of compliments, or the keepers of secrets?

The issue is not of course the appropriateness of such sources. At issue is how to systematically develop and exploit the all-too-often overlooked potential we all have of noting, marking, and reflecting on our own everyday activities. And here is where Systematic Self-Observation has so much to tell us.

ix

Picking up on earlier attempts to chronicle the contours of mundane social life through the use of diaries, time budgets, and highly structured self-reporting schemes, Rodriguez and Ryave develop and illustrate various ways by which self-observations can be situated, aggregated, and thus subjected to analysis. This approach to accounting for—indeed drawing on—the inevitable subjectivity of self-reports owes much to work in ethnomethodology and conversational analysis. And, as Professors Rodriguez and Ryave are quick to suggest, Systematic Self-Observation, like ethnomethodology and conversational analysis, seeks to make visible basic social processes that are everywhere relevant but rarely examined.

J.V.M.
P.K.M.
M.L.M.

FOREWORD

Rodriguez and Ryave's work *Systematic Self-Observation* may be the first of its kind in several ways. This fact is forecasted by the title, for "self-observation" is generally absent from the table of contents or the indexes of typical social science methodology textbooks. Insofar as the topic is mentioned, it receives perhaps a few paragraphs. The "observation" that is spoken about in qualitative sociology and anthropology texts is a series of strategies for being among those you study and doing some things they do while you watch and report on "them." It is not the consistent and direct observation of one's own experience and behavior.

Rodriguez and Ryave present you with an entire book about this subject—explaining what it is and why it is useful and important, and giving clear and practical ways to do it well and accurately.

In one sense, all social science is systematic self-observation in that it is an attempt to study and learn about ourselves. In innumerable ways, this makes it difficult for social scientists to separate subject and object, observer from observed. Whether we like it or not, or want it or not, our "studying" is part of the very social world we study, and it changes that world as well. This basic fact explains why methodology texts have not been brimming with advice on self-observation and why the "scientific" status of social science has remained controversial for over a century.

At one extreme are those who long for the scientific and the objective. They tend to regard the very term *subjective* as a pointer to processes that are inherently prone to bias, error, distortion, and mistake. Much of what they consider methodology is strategies for separating those being studied from those doing the studying, both literally and psychologically.

At the opposite pole are the radical social sciences, consumed with the self-referential paradoxes and empirical problems created by multiple realities constructed from diverse human awareness and consumed by the fact that it is we that study ourselves. They envision the social, human world as a "never-never land" far removed from commonsense notions of reality—a world where observer and observed are always chasing each other's tails and switching roles, where things are both here and not here, where reality is always real and simultaneously socially constructed. These disciplines see little possibility of truth, objectivity, accuracy, and the like in a domain where subject and object must be so linked as to be almost indistinguishable.

This innovative book cuts through this philosophical maze in an immediate and surprisingly unpretentious way. In explaining and tutoring you on their methods of self-observation, the authors deliver a clear message: We *can* learn about our lives while simultaneously living them. If carefully handled, "subjective" experience and self-observation need not be synonymous with bias and error. Such observations can be validated as reliable, valid, and accurate—not always, but far more often than one might suspect. And we need not abandon our commonsense notions of a world that is real and objectively "there" in order to incorporate the varieties of human awareness into social science—as both a tool and a topic of study.

As one of their colleagues, Steven Riskin, suggests, Rodriguez and Ryave, without overly worrying about the logical and philosophical difficulties involved, simply went out and "did it."

The book describes a style of self-observation that has been worked out over a number of years. It is especially valuable at gaining access to phenomena that are not captured by questionnaires, interviews, or direct observation (including videotape). In fact, it opens a whole domain of interesting and important phenomena for research.

—Howard Schwartz, PhD

SYSTEMATIC SELF-OBSERVATION

1. INTRODUCING SYSTEMATIC SELF-OBSERVATION

A renaissance of interest in the qualitative approach to the study of everyday social life is encouraging many researchers to depart from positivistically inspired methods to seek other approaches (Ellis, 1991; Gubrium & Holstein, 1997; Wheeler & Reis, 1991). Systematic Self-Observation (SSO) is a qualitative research strategy that offers researchers access to a virtually unexplored domain. This book provides a description, a theoretical explanation, a set of demonstrations, and a critique of SSO, along with practical guidelines for its application.

Self-observation is an ordinary feature of everyday experience. It has also been used by psychotherapists, educators, and spiritual practitioners for healing, teaching, and promoting self-development. Though features of SSO may be used for these missions (see Chapter 5), this presentation of the method focuses on the contributions it can make to the scientific study of those social and psychological phenomena that are not effectively accessed by conventional research methods. Our 13 years of experience with the application of SSO indicate that it is an adaptable, practical, economic, and productive research strategy.

1

A Brief Description of
Systematic Self-Observation

Systematic Self-Observation involves training informants to observe and record a selected feature of their own everyday experience. SSO training begins with explaining the scientific method and the importance of sensitive observation and data-gathering practices that accurately capture the informants' natural experiences. The researcher then introduces a carefully selected topic for study. The purpose of SSO is to produce accurate descriptions of the informants' experiences.

The researcher instructs the informants to make every effort not to deviate from their natural behavior. They should continue with their lives normally, while alertly observing moments when the research topic occurs. The informants are told to just observe when the phenomenon shows up. For example, when the topic of study was withholding compliments, our informants were told:

> Go about your daily social life as you normally do. Observe when you find yourself withholding a compliment. Do not withhold a compliment on purpose, do not alter your behavior—just observe it.
> Once you become aware that you are withholding a compliment: Do not judge it or question it.
> JUST observe it.

In SSO studies, informants are urged to *immediately* write a field report on their observation, giving a detailed description of the actions and words spoken, along with any background information, thoughts, and emotions that encompass the phenomenon. The field notes should include a description of the situation and the relationships between the people involved. The data set of an SSO study typically includes several reports on the topic by each individual in a group of diverse informants.

The Theoretical and Methodological
Bases for Systematic Self-Observation

Systematic Self-Observation draws much of its inspiration and organizing focus from the theoretical traditions of Erving Goffman, symbolic interactionism, ethnomethodology, semiotics, psycholinguistics, and conversation analysis. Though SSO's connection to these approaches should be of special interest to researchers working in these traditions, it is important to emphasize that SSO can be used for projects far removed from its roots. The

SSO method is a research tool that can be readily and productively applied to a wide range of subject matters and theoretical paradigms. Given this admonition, the following discussion of the theoretical presumptions and practical concerns that inspired and formed SSO more fully explicates the method.

SSO emerged from the conviction that it is the understanding of the ordinary that is problematic. Researchers from many different traditions have determined that distinct and important insights into social life can be acquired through the study of the multitude of small events of everyday life (see Goffman, 1959, 1967; Reis & Wheeler, 1991). The research program that inspired the development of SSO was the quest to discover, describe, and understand the detailed order of ordinary life as it is experienced.

Many important psychological and social phenomena can be observed only by the person having the experience (Schwartz & Jacobs, 1979). For example, Goffman's (1959) study of "backstage" and "camouflaged" social behaviors recognizes that observable displays are only part of social reality. Overt behavior often hides many important phenomena. The special contribution of SSO is the access it gives to covert, elusive, and/or personal experiences like cognitive processes, emotions, motives, concealed actions, omitted actions, and socially restricted activities.

According to Sacks (1992), when the scientific endeavor is to discover, describe, and analyze everyday social phenomena, researchers should remain descriptively close to the phenomena and try to use conceptualizations that have an everyday intelligibility. Similarly, Psathas (1995) has recommended "the avoidance of preformulated theoretical or conceptual categories and the adoption of an open-mindedness and a willingness to be led by the phenomena of study" (p. 2). Thus, ordinary, mundane topics are recommended. For example, some of the everyday life topics that we have researched with SSO have been lies (a case study of concealed actions), secrets (a case study of restricted actions), the withholding of compliments (a case study of withheld actions), the occasions when individuals compare themselves to another (a case study of thought processes), and the experience of envy (a case study of an emotion). Synopses of these studies are found in Chapter 4.

The subject matter for SSO studies is nicely identified in Max Weber's (1967) definition of social conduct, which includes the study of subjective meaning, mental "behaviors," and nonactions:

> Human behavior shall be called "conduct" when, and in so far as, the person or persons acting combine with their behavior some subjective meaning. The behavior may be mental or external; it may consist in action or the omission to

act. Conduct will be called "social conduct" where its intention is related by the actor or actors to the conduct of others and oriented accordingly in its course. (p. 1)

Social life should be documented and analyzed from the perspective and level from which it is produced. The conscious or unconscious (theoretical) assumptions of the researcher can miss, block out, or contaminate the meanings that participants give to their own activities and experiences. Thus, SSO data are expressed in the informants' own voices.

SSO data produce firsthand accounts of events because the observed and the observer are the same person. The meanings, perspective, and feelings in the data are exactly what the researcher wants to know. By contrast, traditional participant and nonparticipant observation methods produce field notes that are secondhand accounts. These are influenced by the researcher's personal perspective and theoretical style (Silverman, 1993). In traditional studies, the researcher's observations and field notes are a construction that remains unanalyzed (Garfinkel & Sacks, 1970; Sacks, 1963).

The problem of the researcher's imprint on the *raw* data can sometimes be resolved with the use of audio- and videotape recordings, where the tapes and transcripts of those tapes replace field notes. But conventional observation methods can't observe and tape-record the many important hidden and elusive aspects of people's lives.

Interviews and questionnaires are the conventional methods for gathering data on meanings, perceptions, attitudes, thought processes, emotions, and concealed, socially restricted, and omitted actions or nonactions. But researchers have developed serious reservations about using interviews and questionnaires to study these processes of everyday social life. The literature on social cognition is filled with studies showing how difficult it is to remember specific qualities of mundane occurrences (Markus & Zajonc, 1985). Likewise, anthropologists, psychologists, and sociological researchers who study ordinary, everyday experiences and interactions observe that many features go unnoticed and unremembered (Schutz, 1962). Even when informants are cooperative and honest, many activities are done in such a taken-for-granted, habituated, and/or unconscious manner that they are unavailable for recall.

The insights of ethnomethodology and Polanyi's (1967) understanding of the *tacit dimension* explain why individuals are unable to be aware of, or remember, many features of experience. A numbness to the details of everyday life is required for the competent achievement of socially skillful behavior (Polanyi, 1967). For example, our initial research attempt used conventional interviews, asking people to *recall* the lies they told in everyday life. This research yielded limited results because the interviewees were hardly able to recollect the lies they told, other than the ones that were elaborately premeditated.

Using SSO, not only do our informants observe that they are doing a different type of lying but they are quite amazed at how frequently they are telling lies in their everyday interactions. The lies they tell and the details in which the lies are situated are partially obscured in the tacit dimension. Many lies become observable only when the informants are instructed ahead of time to self-observe them.

The goal of the SSO method is to generate field notes that are accurate descriptions of the participants' experience. Social life is a complex, situated, occasioned, fast-paced, and improvised stream of phenomena that unfolds from moment to moment. A rigorous research strategy must take into account the huge complexity, the partial visibility, and the dynamic pace of natural life, as well as the fact that informants are both social players and observers, experiencing complex demands. For these reasons, an SSO topic should be a *single, focused* phenomenon that is *natural* to the culture, is readily *noticeable*, is *intermittent* (as opposed to chronically occurring), is *bounded* (has a beginning and an ending), and is of *short duration*. The field notes describe the experiences in the informants' own words and from their own personal points of view.

A Brief Review of Social Science Endeavors at Self-Observation

In the early 20th century, there was a wave of behaviorist, positivist, and objectivist trends in the social sciences (Hinkle & Hinkle, 1954; Schwartz & Jacobs, 1979; Watson, 1913; Wheeler & Reis, 1991). These trends dismissed subjective experience, introspection, and the study of the details of everyday life experiences as too "soft," vague, or idiosyncratic to be the appropriate subject matter for rigorous social scientific investigation.

The social fact paradigm was countered by seminal contributors to the social sciences who relied on self-observation as part of their methodological base. (consider, e.g., Cooley, 1926; Dilthey, 1976; Garfinkel, 1967; Goffman, 1967; Jung, 1961; Weber, 1949; Znaniecki, 1934). Some social philosophers and psychologists like Heidegger, Husserl, George Herbert Mead, Merleau-Ponty, and Wundt also used some form of introspection as their fundamental method (Ellis, 1991).

Though some contemporary social scientists openly count self-observation as a legitimate source of information and insight, in actual practice, it is a deliberately unacknowledged or simply unconscious adjunct to *all* other methods of data collection (Caughey, 1982, 1984; Crapanzano, 1970; Denzin, 1971; Ellis, 1991; Grover, 1982; Johnson, 1975; Krieger, 1985; Singer, 1966; Wallace, 1972). But since the 1970s, there have been a number of efforts to harness self-observation as a social science research method.

Those researchers who have explored self-observation research strategies share several features. They tend to be interested in studying human behavior as it naturally occurs. They are concerned with gaining empirical information on the detailed aspects of everyday life. Finally, they justify their use of self-observation by noting the inadequacy of commonly used social science methods for accessing these kinds of subject matter.

Although there are common features to the various research practices of self-observation, certain variables can be used to contrast these methods. First, *who* does the self-observing—researchers or informants? Second, *what* is to be observed? The theoretical orientation of the researcher who shapes the research question largely determines the formulation of the topic. The phenomena to be observed have ranged from singular topics (particular activities, thoughts, or emotions) to whole complexes of actions, or even the organization of a whole day's activities. Finally, *how* is the experience of self-observation to be transformed into data? Self-reported field notes, narratives, diaries, tape recordings, questionnaires, interviews, or some combination of these have been used to form the database.

A distinctive theme of self-observation research is that the researcher analyzes her or his own experience. In many of these efforts, the line between data and analysis is blurred. In *Ways of the Hand* (1978), David Sudnow self-observed and introspected on his practice and experience in playing jazz piano. He used this analysis as a metaphor for describing the improvisational features of human interaction and communication. Carolyn Ellis (1991) used her own self-introspection narratives to study emotions. Jerome Singer (1975) self-observed and analyzed his own daydreams as the initial part of his report on this subjective and elusive topic.

In his paper "Driving to Work," Anthony Wallace (1972) demonstrated that self-observation can be used by anthropologists to study their own society. Using self-observation, he attempted to make explicit the tacit cognitive processes that he used to drive from home to work. Though acknowledging this effort as interesting and innovative, David Hayano (1979) questioned the generalizability of Wallace's cognitive rules because they were based on a sample size of only one. However, sample size becomes relevant only in light of the subject matter being studied. If the phenomenon under study is generic, a small sample will suffice. But the universality of the phenomenon is an empirical question that only more research will begin to resolve. It has been more common for social scientists to recruit many informants to make observations, and this has been true for SSO as well. In most informant-based self-observation studies, the phenomena studied and the manner of reporting are strongly influenced by the researcher's theoretical orientation (Duck, 1991). When informants generate the body of data, the distinction between the data and the analysis of the data can be more clearly drawn.

Ellis (1991) argued for a method of "systematic sociological introspection" as an appropriate method for studying everyday emotional life. She not only proposed self-introspection but also introduced the strategy that she called "interactive introspection." In this format, the researcher and subject interview one another as equals who try to help one another relive and describe their recollection of emotional experiences. Both the researcher's and the informant's descriptions of their emotional experiences constitute the database.

In their ethnographic study of counterculture youth, Wieder and Zimmerman (1977) used a diary-interview method as a more economic alternative to direct observation. Their informants were asked to record, in chronological order, the daily activities they engaged in over the course of 7 days with the researchers' format of "Who/What/When/Where/How?" along with instructions to avoid omitting events because they seemed mundane. "We inveighed them to be frank and include such things as sexual activity and drug use. We asked them to be as detailed as they could and suggested that they set aside regular periods during the day to write the diary" (pp. 486-487). Afterward, the researchers reviewed the diary as the source of questions for a follow-up interview to expand the data by filling in details and leading beyond events to "attitude, belief, knowledge and experience of a more general character" (p. 491). This ethnographic approach is suited for capturing a broad overview of a cultural group.

Singer and Kolligian (1987; cited in Genest & Turk, 1981) studied private experience both in the controlled laboratory setting and in the ordinary course of daily life. Their methodological strategy is striking because sometimes they asked the participants to talk out loud, reflecting on their thought processes.

Wheeler and Reis (1991) categorized three types of self-recording methods developed by social psychologists interested in the details of daily life: (a) interval-, (b) signal-, and (c) event-contingent recording. Each uses self-observation, asking subjects to make a record of situated features of their daily lives.

1. *Interval-Contingent Recording*: Zautra, Finch, Reich, and Guarnaccia (1991) had all their participating subjects write a self-report at a predetermined interval (e.g., every 4 hours), describing the details of a predetermined subject (e.g., mood) since the last reporting interval. These self-reported descriptions were elicited by questionnaires rather than narratives. The interval-contingent method is effective for studying the frequency of selected daily life events or to characterize details of experience over some designated time period.

2. *Signal-Contingent Recording*: Wong and Csikszentmihalyi (1991) asked their informants to stop and describe their experiences whenever they were signaled to do so by the researcher. Most studies involve six to nine signals a day, and the timing of the signals is unknown to the subjects. The accounts that are given immediately after the signal are elicited by a structured questionnaire. An advantage of this method is the proximity in time between the signal-initiated self-observing and the reporting by the informant. This practice is useful for sampling cognitive and/or emotional states and practical activities during everyday activities.

3. *Event-Contingent Recording*: The Rochester Interaction Record (Reis & Wheeler, 1991; Wheeler & Nezlek, 1977) asks the self-observing subjects to complete a report any time some event occurs that meets a predetermined definition. For example, for every social encounter lasting 10 minutes or longer, participating subjects are asked to fill out a standardized, fixed-format questionnaire. The questionnaire may feature scaled items that ask the informants to evaluate an interaction's "intimacy" on a scale from 1 (*superficial*) to 7 (*meaningful*) (Wheeler, Reis, & Nezlek, 1983). The Iowa Interaction Record (Duck & Rutt, 1988) also uses a quantified scaled questionnaire with items like "This was just talk for talk's sake" that are rated from 1 (*strong agreement*) to 9 (*strong disagreement*). The Rochester and Iowa Interaction Record indices are useful for studying selected domains of interaction by focusing on specific predefined issues and for collecting a large database.

Anthropologist John Caughey (1982, 1984), working in the area of American studies, explores thought processes such as dreams, fantasies, stream of consciousness, idealizations of media figures, hallucinations, and delusions in *Imaginary Social Worlds* (1984). Caughey pointed out that the *only* way to obtain data on such processes is through asking one's subjects to introspect.

How Systematic Self-Observation Contrasts
With the Other Self-Observation Methods

Caughey's (1984) approach fits the Systematic Self-Observation paradigm, with the only difference being that his choice of subject matter (fantasies) is possibly too demanding for beginning self-observers. He used his students as informants and had them write narrative field notes when they noticed that they had just engaged in a fantasy. The self-observation reports of his informants constituted the database that enabled Caughey to study fantasies of everyday life. Because fantasies are multidimensional, vague, ubiquitous, and largely embedded in the tacit dimension, capturing and reporting such an unfocused phenomenon could be a daunting task for an informant. It is encouraging that Caughey reported that most students were able to produce detailed accounts of their fantasies.

SSO also differs from Ellis's (1991) method of "interactive introspection." In SSO, the interaction between researcher and informant comes to an end *before* the data are gathered.

SSO is an event-contingent method because the natural emergence of the targeted topic triggers the observing and reporting. Its database greatly differs from that produced by Wieder and Zimmerman's (1977) instructions to write a diary including "everything that was notable" in a day's activities. By contrast, SSO is a very focused form of self-observation. The SSO approach asks the informant to stay mindfully attentive—watching for the natural occurrence of *a particular kind of event.* Moreover, the time gap between the natural occurrence of the activity to be observed and the write-up of the field notes is minimized by SSO in that the informants are asked to write their report *immediately* after the observation.

In contrast with the Rochester and Iowa Interaction Records' event-contingent questionnaires, the SSO method has the informant write a narrative. The only structuring of the field notes is the instructions to identify the *situation,* the *participants,* and what occurred, including the *words spoken and/or any thoughts and feelings* that the informant had. Because the researcher asks informants to respond to these features of their experience, SSO could be characterized as an event-contingent, open-ended self-interview, eliciting a description of experience that is drawn from direct observation.

The SSO format generates data closer to the naturally experienced event because the informants identify the occurrence of the phenomenon and because the data are the informants' own descriptions. In contrast to research methods that use a preformulated questionnaire that directs the informants' observations (and thus imposes an ordering of experience that is the researcher's conception), SSO generates data that are written in the informants' own words and marked with their unique personal sensibilities, voices, perspectives, experiences, and points of view.

SSO strives for scientific rigor. It is a flexible research strategy that is intended to maximize the quality and validity of the descriptions generated through self-observation.

2. IMPLEMENTING SYSTEMATIC SELF-OBSERVATION

This chapter describes and discusses the application of Systematic Self-Observation (SSO). It also identifies options for researchers who seek to adapt the SSO method to their own research purposes. Finally, it discusses ethical considerations and presents an evaluation of the method.

The logic of the SSO strategy is the result of efforts to maximize rigorous research standards while adapting to the practical problems involved in studying everyday life through self-observation.

An SSO study involves the following sequence of tasks:

1. Choosing a subject matter that is appropriate for the SSO method
2. Formulating the topic
3. Recruiting informants
4. Guiding informants to understand and appreciate the logic of social scientific inquiry in the research project
5. Teaching informants to be sensitive, reliable, and accurate observers
6. Teaching informants to report their observations in a detailed and accurate manner
7. Preparing the informants with training exercises

Choosing the Subject Matter for Study

Everyday social life is made up of overwhelming details of experience. To address this complexity, a research topic should clearly identify a focused phenomenon that is both theoretically and practically suited for self-observation.

Not all social and psychological activities or experiences are appropriate for Systematic Self-Observation. For example, the study of the overt domain of social actions, like the conversational activities of complimenting, insulting, and complaining, will yield more valid and reliable data with a tape recorder. SSO is more appropriate for the study of hidden or elusive domains, like the motives, memories, thought processes, withheld actions, thoughts, and/or emotions that accompany overt behaviors. Some form of self-observation may be the best way—or the only way—to gather data on these phenomena because they are hidden and subjective.

In choosing a topic, researchers should take into account the practical problem of capturing the ongoing, routinized, tacit, and elusive nature of natural social life. The researcher's choice of topic should take into consideration the fact that informants must be able to reliably notice, sensitively observe, and accurately reconstruct their observations into field notes without interfering with the process of the social event.

A primary goal of researchers who study everyday life is to discover the order and organization that shapes natural life experiences and activities. The choice of the topic for an SSO study is itself an act of analysis that begins to contribute to the researcher's description of the phenomenon. Choosing a *single* topic gives the SSO research a theoretical focus. This makes the research task practical, and operates to make visible the tacit domain of behavior and experience. A good topic enables the observer to cut through all the buzzing details of social experience to cast the spotlight on a taken-for-granted and routinized feature of life that would normally remain obscured and in the background of awareness.

The less abstract and the more concrete the topic for self-observation, the more likely it is that the research will capture and report the phenomenon. For example, the topic of Reis and Wheeler's (1991) study, "interactions that last more than 10 minutes," does not spotlight any particular behavior, so the habituated and taken-for-granted activities in the 10 minutes are likely to remain tacit and unnoticed in the informants' experiences and reports. This vagueness of topic ultimately limits the researchers' ability to identify and describe an underlying order in their analysis (Katz, 1999).

A topic should be *specific*. For example, if the researcher is interested in studying intimacy, an assignment to report instances of "admitting to someone that you are afraid of something" (a more specific feature of intimacy) is more likely to yield detailed and analytically rich data than a vague and general assignment to report instances of "being open" or "moments of social intimacy." Similarly, a study of moments in everyday life when one is "acting" is likely to yield less reliable, valid, or analytically accessible data than a more focused study on "acting dumb" or "acting upset."

Chronically recurring, long-lasting, or diffuse phenomena can present an overly demanding data collection task. For example, pervasive thoughts like "anticipations" are probably too omnipresent to be observed and accurately reported for a sustained period of time by most informants. Longer-lasting activities like extended daydreams are difficult to accurately and sensitively observe and report. Because many people have recurrent and/or extended flights of fantasy, some of Caughey's (1984) informants were confronted with a daunting self-observational task. Unbounded or diffuse topics like "acting friendly" or "feeling unsure" make it hard for the informant to identify when an activity or experience begins and/or ends.

For practical reasons, the topic should be a phenomenon that occurs *intermittently* (as opposed to occurring more chronically), is *bounded* (has an identifiable beginning and end), and is of *short duration*. Research from the field of cognitive psychology supports these recommendations. Studies show that people do not remember the details of events unless they plan ahead to pay attention to those details specifically (Nickerson & Adams, 1979). Schneider and Shiffrin (1977) demonstrated that perception improves when the targeted phenomena are few and similar.

Another strategy for managing the work of an SSO study is to restrict self-observations to particular settings or to certain relationships. Broad research topics like "withholding criticism," "responding to and/or producing gossip," or "feeling put down" may be more manageable and informative if the assignment is limited to selected settings such as work, school, or recreational settings or to interactions with particular types of relationships such as those with friends, family, clients, or staff. (Specifying the relationships surrounding the observation may be of special value in therapeutic applications of SSO, discussed in Chapter 5.)

The SSO recommendations for choosing a topic are intended to make the three tasks of recognizing, self-observing, and reporting the background details of everyday life more manageable—and thus more likely to yield reliable and valid qualitative data. The recommendation to select a focused (single, concrete, specific, intermittent, bounded, short) topic for study is *not* intended to yield a precise definition or to generate a unit of measurement of the phenomenon. The study of the covert and tacit realms of social phenomena is in an exploratory stage of development. The quest to describe and understand the nature of these domains turns on questions about "what" is occurring rather than "how much." Quantitative concerns about the frequency of a certain phenomenon may be less relevant than capturing a unique datum that reveals the underlying meaning and motivational organization of a phenomenon.[1]

Chapter 5 provides a list of potentially researchable topics, along with suggestions for generating SSO topics.

Formulating the Topic

Theoretical as well as practical considerations suggest that the topic given to the informants be expressed in the vernacular. Researchers should avoid abstract academic language and should choose a recognizable feature of ordinary experience that captures the meaning systems of real life (Kirk & Miller, 1986). Artificial, preformulated topics (and research instruments, like questionnaires, that are the vehicles for those formulations) impose the researcher's system of meaning on the data (Cicourel, 1964). Although this may be appropriate for certain types of studies, it deviates from the goal of problematizing the ordinary and trying to capture, describe, and analyze the detailed order embedded in the natural occurrences of everyday life (Psathas, 1995).

Researchable topics vary in how well their wording is grounded in the vernacular. Mundane phenomena that are described without jargon—for example, "telling lies," "telling secrets," "regretting how something 'came out,'" "making a fool of yourself," "taking criticism," "putdowns," "name dropping," "bluffing," and "feeling sad over another's success"—are more likely to be noticed because they are part of people's natural language and experience. A technical topic like "social comparison processes" needs to be translated into "occasions when you find yourself observing someone else and you start comparing yourself to that other person" and thereafter referred to simply as "self-other comparisons."

Leaving a topic imprecisely defined encourages people to employ their own understanding of it. Garfinkel (1967) demonstrated that the vagueness of natural language is a necessary feature of its practical communicativeness. Using the imprecise language of everyday life has been a successful strategy in that our informants have not needed formal definitions of topics to observe the phenomena in their lives.

The value of the option of giving no definitions, and thus inviting the informants to use their own understanding of the topic, is illustrated in our SSO study of secrets told in everyday life. When given the assignment to self-observe secrets, a few individuals asked for a definition of "a secret." We evaded the issue by responding to the request for a definition with "whatever 'a secret' means to you." As a result, we discovered that there are two types: *explicit secrets* (that start or conclude with an explicit statement that frames the information as exclusive, such as "It's a secret," "This is confidential," or "Don't tell anyone") and *implicit secrets*. Implicit secrets occur when the informant just "knows" by the private nature of the information and/or by the manner in which it was delivered that the information is "a secret." If we had given a definition or an example of an explicit secret to the informants, the data set might have excluded the implicit secrets. Instead, our strategy allowed for empirically generated definitions.

Researchers should also encourage informants to take the broadest possible interpretation of the topic. A single exceptional datum may provide the analytic template that reveals the hidden order or organization of the phenomenon (Katz, 1999; Kirk & Miller, 1986; Psathas, 1995). (For an example in this book of the theoretical value of a single exceptional case, see Chapter 4, the section "Case Study 1: Telling Lies in Everyday Life," subsection "A Deviant Case Clinches the Analysis.")

Examples have the potential to fixate, bias, taint, or limit the informant's perception. Examples can be especially prejudicial if they become the most powerful way that the topic becomes formulated in the minds of the informants. If a topic is not familiar or obvious, and examples seem necessary, then the researcher may want to flood the informants with many and diverse types of examples.

However, if the informants apparently have a clear enough sense of the topic, the researcher may want to give no examples. We gave no examples in our study of self-other comparisons, and there was a virtual absence of two of the four possible kinds of evaluative social comparisons: People rarely reported that they felt "equal" or just "different." Our informants overwhelmingly made hierarchical comparisons in which they felt "better" or "worse." Had the four types been presented as examples, this significant finding might have been minimized or obscured.

The instructions should emphasize the importance of including all questionable instances. We tell our informants, *"If you're in any way in doubt, always write it up and turn it in."* It is always possible to exclude misconstrued observations, but a marginal instance that is not reported could be an invaluable loss.

In sum, SSO topics should be of single, hidden, or elusive phenomena that are concrete, specific, intermittently occurring, bounded, of short duration, presented in the vernacular, and without extended definitions or limiting examples. After the fieldwork, researchers may want to allow their inductive analysis of the data to contribute to the description and definition of the topic.

Because every research topic and purpose is unique, all of these recommendations are offered as considerations. The issues involved in deciding how the topic is presented to informants will be more fully articulated as studies yield feedback on these options.

Recruiting Informants

Self-observation is a practical activity involving various skills that are not equally distributed. Some informants will be more sensitive and insightful than others. Ideally, the Systematic Self-Observation researcher should recruit and train a large and diverse sample of informants, located in many diverse situations, in order to broaden the database and increase the potential for deviant case analyses (Silverman, 1993).[2]

Anthropologists make heavy use of informant-based research, but they have yet to recruit informants to *systematically* self-observe and report on the hidden and elusive features of everyday life. A presentation of our study of "the lies told in everyday life" to an audience of sociologists at Nihon University in Tokyo elicited a strong reaction. Because Americans appear so blunt, the Japanese sociologists were quite surprised to learn that Americans lied in similar ways and for similar reasons.[3] Their reaction suggests that some of the features of everyday life that can be investigated by SSO could be cultural universals with interesting variations that wait to be studied. Because SSO studies can be used by anthropologists for comparative studies, SSO informants can be recruited from any culture.

Like many studies in the social sciences, our SSO research, to date, has drawn informants from students enrolled in sociology courses on our respective campuses. SSO is a compelling academic assignment. Although taking part in an SSO exercise is anonymous and optional, students rarely elect not to participate.

The classes in Los Angeles had a predominance of white, black, Chicano, older, and more urban students. The sociology classes at the more rurally based campus in Hawaii had a predominance of younger, Asian American, Hawaiian, Portuguese, and Pacific Islander students. Despite the broad diversity in age, race, ethnicity, and region of residence of the combined sample of our informants, there was great consistency in the data. This finding suggests the generic quality of the phenomena that can be investigated using SSO. In the final analysis, the research purpose determines the types of people who constitute an appropriate pool of informants.

A researcher should meet with the recruited informants as a group so that all informants receive the same instructions. The prefieldwork contact with informants is the researcher's primary opportunity to influence and direct the data-gathering practices that thereafter will be occurring outside the researcher's purview.

Guiding Informants to
Be Scientific Observers

Next to selecting the topic for study, the most important task of the researcher is to train the informants to become reliable and accurate observers and reporters. The researcher should seek to inculcate the informants with research attitudes and skills that will optimize the quality of the data. Informant-based research requires willingness on the part of the informants to conscientiously cooperate, but the informants' understanding, motivation, and skills cannot be assumed.

The *attitude of informants* is critical. Do the informants take the task seriously? Do they appreciate the importance of empirically based knowledge? Do they comprehend what it means to reliably and validly observe and write up their observations? Do they understand that sensitivity to details is important? Do they understand how the value of the research endeavor rises or falls depending on the quality of their reports?

The researcher can impart the right attitude by introducing the informants to some of the canons of science. The informants should be taught the significance of data-based knowledge and the concepts of validity, reliability, and scientific rigor. In short, informants should be encouraged to be honest, consistently mindful of their task, sensitive to detail, and accurate.

Teaching Informants How to Observe

How should the informants approach their task? When the goal is to study the phenomena of everyday life in their natural expressions, informants should be told to *go about their daily life as they normally do and in no way to act differently as a result of the assignment*. Informants are warned *not* to purposely produce the phenomenon under investigation. They should be reminded that they have by no means failed if they simply observe that they never engaged in the activity or experience. The observation of the absence of the phenomenon is just as important and is worth reporting.

The informants should be instructed to act differently in only one way: They are to try to be mindfully attentive so that they can notice those occasions when they experience the targeted phenomenon. Awareness is crucial for the successful implementation of SSO.

Once the phenomenon is noticed, informants are instructed not to alter its production. Taking a cue from psychotherapeutic and spiritual practices, informants are emphatically instructed *not to judge* the propriety or the morality of the occurrence of the phenomenon being self-observed (Beck, 1989; Hanh, 1987; Rogers, 1961). The instructions to the informant are: *"Once*

you notice that it [the topic] is happening: do not judge it, do not slow down,
do not speed up, do not change it, do not question it—just observe it."
   Informants are then given a set period of time to conduct their self-
observations. The decision about the proper time period depends on the
topic, the social context, and the researcher's purposes. In our SSO studies,
the time period ranged from 2 days to 2 weeks. In that time period, informants are instructed to observe and record *all* experiences of the phenomenon. On occasion, as a mnemonic device, informants wear a rubber band or
tie a string around their wrist. As they go about their daily activities, the
string reminds them to be ready to recognize the phenomenon if/when it
occurs.

Teaching Informants How
to Report Self-Observations

   Although the method of Systematic Self-Observation shares an event-
contingent approach with the Rochester Interaction Record, it differs on
the nature of the reporting required once the event has been noticed. The
Rochester and Iowa studies ask informants to complete standardized,
fixed-format questionnaires (Reis & Wheeler, 1991; Wheeler et al., 1983).
By contrast, SSO asks for relatively unstructured narrative field notes. This
approach encourages description of the event in the informant's voice.
   The field notes should *only* describe what happened. They should not
revise or evaluate the activity or experience in any way. Informants must
understand that in the data-gathering stage their interpretation, analysis,
understanding, or appreciation of the topic—unless it is part of the observed
experience—is inappropriate (Katz, 1999). Informants should be told not to
place a moral judgment on the self-observed phenomenon unless this was
part of the original experience. Field notes should be done honestly, carefully, and in detail. In short, the informant should strive only to be a reliable and accurate recorder, describing the phenomenon exactly as it was
experienced.
   Because the time lapse between the observation and the writing of the
report should be minimized, the informants should carry pencil and paper
and fully write a description of the event *immediately* or as soon as it is practically possible.[4]
   The informants must include the following in their field notes: a descriptive construction of (a) *the situation* in which the activity occurred; (b) the
relationships of *the participants* (using social roles and fictitious names);
and (c) a careful reconstruction of *the words spoken, and the informants'*

thoughts and feelings. Depending on the research goal, the researchers may want to introduce additional field note requirements.

To avoid imposing a preconceived order on the data, the researcher gives no additional details as to how the informants should format their field notes. This loose structure, along with the variability in informants' diligence and skill, results in data that come with different formats, details, and sensitivity.

Because of ethical considerations, and to discourage self-censorship and phony reports, informants are instructed to keep their field notes *anonymous.* The researchers should make every effort to protect the anonymity of all parties—the informants and those they report on. We also assure informants that their reports will not be evaluated or graded. Any informant can refuse to participate or withdraw from the research without being penalized or even identified. She or he need only hand in a blank paper. However, if informants participated but did not observe the phenomenon, they are told to report that. The decisions to maintain anonymity and/or not to grade the reports are optional.

Preparing Informants With Training Exercises

Our experience with Systematic Self-Observation research indicates that an informant's motivation and capacity to self-observe improves with practice. The spiritual and therapeutic literature on self-observation corroborates that the self-observation of thoughts and behaviors without judgment or alteration and the reporting of those observations are skills that grow with practice (Beck, 1989; Hanh, 1987; Kornfield, 1993).

Our experience has taught us that a few practice SSO exercises can sharpen the informants' self-observing skills. We recommend the study of lies as a training exercise. This can be followed by practice exercises on the observation of verbalized activities of longer duration (like secrets) and then exercises on the observation of nonverbalized thoughts, emotions, and covert behaviors like withheld compliments, self-other comparisons, and envy.

We have given our students the assignment of analyzing their class's data set. This theory-building assignment tends to enhance their consciousness and skill as informants because it can show the importance of accurate and detailed reports. We frequently use the following datum from the original lies study to demonstrate the importance of noticing and reporting details like pauses, vocalizations, and capturing the exact language used. In the following example, the "Um" (which is a pause) and the "okay" (which is a "downplayed acceptance") reveal the ambivalence that motivates the lie in the following instance:

Place: Hilo Apartment.
Who: Boyfriend and me.
Situation: Trying to decide what we were to do this evening.

Me: So what are we going to do?
Boyfriend: Wanna go bowling tonight?
Me: Um, okay. [LIE] How long do you want to bowl?
Boyfriend: Well, would you prefer to see a movie tonight?
Me: Yes. Let's go to a movie instead.

After completing an exercise with a full round of instructions, data collection, and analysis, the informants are appreciably more interested, motivated, and skilled at SSO. With this training, they are well prepared for a new topic for SSO.

Ethical Considerations

We preserve our informants' privacy by instructing them to keep their identity and the identities of other participants anonymous. The description and analysis of the order and organization of everyday social life are not dependent on personalities. To date, our inability to connect field notes to specific individuals has not been problematic for our work, and it has probably increased the honesty and validity of our data.

Systematic Self-Observation produces reports of what people are naturally, readily, and typically doing. Their behavior is not likely to change for the worse from having participated in a SSO assignment. Informants will probably continue to tell lies, engage in secret-telling interactions, experience self-other comparisons, and withhold compliments in much the same way, despite their enhanced awareness of these processes.

The psychological impact that SSO might have on informants is an ethical concern. SSO was developed to generate data on neglected and obscure topics of social life. Our SSO studies have exposed some of the hostile undercuts of the social and psychological features of everyday life. Informants increase their awareness of the lies they tell, the times they withhold praise or feel happy over another's misfortune, and so on. Along with revealing some altruistic motives, informants' field notes uncover covert, duplicitous, hostile, competitive, and manipulative activities. Might informants be observing more than they are ready for?

We have little evidence of harm coming from greater awareness of social psychological processes. The alternate possibility that such awareness may be beneficial is discussed in Chapter 5. In our SSO studies, many have been amazed at what they observed about their own life, yet only a handful have reported acute astonishment. For example, students have said, "It's a shock to realize that I'm going around telling lies all day!" but no one has reported experiencing extended personal distress.

Some topics that SSO could open to layperson informants may be challenging to some individuals. Although we have had no problems in 13 years of using SSO in our colleges, we are still concerned about the possibility that informants could react negatively. Increased self-awareness of a sensitive topic for a predisposed individual might degenerate into self-recriminations and judgmental self-consciousness. As a precaution, the possibility of a negative reaction should be considered ahead of time, along with a plan for how the researcher might identify and deal with a disturbed informant.

Feedback on Systematic Self-Observation

Feedback on the Systematic Self-Observation method emerged from our own self-observations and from discussions with informants after various research projects.

We have found that recruiting students from college classes in the social sciences to act as informants has both provided valuable data and been a sound pedagogy. Students are especially suited to do informant-based research because they tend to be literate, teachable, cooperative, motivated, and sensitive observers. The SSO research strategy is especially suitable for academic researchers because SSO studies are economical in terms of both time and money.

Almost all informants were able to notice the research topic that was assigned, even in the studies where no definitions and/or examples were provided. Informants overwhelmingly reported that, with practice, they improved their capacity to unobtrusively observe themselves while participating in an interaction.

The most significant feedback we received was that most informants said they had no trouble just observing the activity without interfering with or altering its production. They told us that being unobtrusive was easy because they typically noticed the occurrence of the topic in midstream or just after it had occurred. Moreover, informants noted that the phenomenon they observed had its own path and timing that was not derailed by being observed.

They reported "a habitlike progression," "a momentum," "naturalness," and "normal[cy]" in the phenomenon.

The feedback from our informants shows that many natural social activities, though spontaneous and improvised, are also routinized and habituated actions (Sudnow, 1978). Theoretical insights as well as research evidence indicate that interaction processes have their own momentum and inertia (Ellis, 1991; Harre, 1986; Hochschild, 1983; Katz, 1999). The feedback from our informants also provides grounds for thinking that for many topics, the SSO method is not reactive; that is, it is not altering the phenomena it is studying.

Informants regularly reported that they were "surprised" at the frequency and the various ways that the topic naturally occurred in their daily lives. For example, informants were surprised by how often they lied, the many times and different ways they compared themselves to other people, and the particular people from whom they withheld compliments. These feelings of surprise, and the sense of new awareness of the phenomena under study, are significant for two reasons. First, they support the contention that conventional social science methods of interrogation that use retrospection (e.g., questionnaires and interviews) are inadequate for recalling the taken-for-granted details of everyday social life. Second, they show that SSO is able to access the routinized, habituated, and semiconscious tacit dimension of personal and social life.

Not only have our SSO studies focused on numerous topics, but these studies have been successfully replicated with different samples of informants. These findings demonstrate reliability and suggest that general features of social life are being identified.

Although there are indications that SSO is a viable scientific method that can generate potentially valuable data, the method also raises perplexing problems. These methodological issues are the focus of the next chapter.

3. A CRITICAL EVALUATION OF SYSTEMATIC SELF-OBSERVATION

An evaluation of the scientific merit of a research method depends on a critical analysis of the procedures it employs and the quality of the data that it generates. Systematic Self-Observation (SSO) should be evaluated in terms of the scientific standards of validity and reliability and the related concern to avoid error and bias in the data it produces.

Validity refers to the extent to which the data set actually captures what is being studied. Kirk and Miller (1986) explained that technically speaking, the use of the term *validity* is a hedged synonym for "the truth." Every scientific method ultimately strives to achieve valid measurement.

Reliability refers to the extent to which the method generates consistent results. Reliability is measured by the sameness or similarity of the data produced (Kirk & Miller, 1986), but reliability alone does not automatically mean that the measurement is valid.

Bias is a systematic influence that "slants" the data in some direction. It is a dangerous form of error because the influence may be invisible and can lead to a consistent (reliable) but false picture of the phenomenon being studied. "Errors" differ from bias in that simple errors will occur at random, whereas a bias is a systematic error that skews the data.

In this chapter, we identify some possible sources of bias in the use of SSO. Though some problems can be addressed, others raise perplexing questions about the data.

SSO, as a practical activity, proceeds in four stages: The researcher chooses the informants, the researcher gives the informants research instructions, the informants observe the target phenomenon, and the informants write up their observations. We discuss possible sources of error and bias for each of these stages.

Problems in Choosing the Informants

One can always challenge the representativeness of a sample. Our Systematic Self-Observation studies have drawn informants from college students enrolled in sociology classes, but the resulting analyses implicitly generalize to the broader society. The representativeness of college students is a concern.

The adequacy of a sample depends on the actual distribution of the phenomenon being studied in the larger population. If the phenomenon is generic, then even a very small and unique group can be a representative sample. For example, a sewing circle in Mississippi may be a representative sample if the topic is observance of American holidays but an unrepresentative sample for the study of the use of swearwords.

In the replications of our studies of lies, withheld compliments, self-other comparisons, pretending not to notice, telling a secret, and so forth, the data have been consistently similar, familiar, and ordinary. The informants readily recognize themselves in one another's field notes. The particular college populations that we have drawn from for these SSO studies are extraordinarily diverse with regard to such variables as age, race, ethnicity, section of the country, and urbanity. Despite these differences, the findings have remained remarkably consistent, suggesting that these social activities are general features of social life and that such conventional distinctions as social class, race, gender, and ethnicity are analytically marginal for our research topics.

Because different types of people tended to participate in the social world in very similar ways with regard to the topics we studied, conventional sampling concerns may not apply to some of the subject matter appropriate to SSO studies. Future research that drops anonymity and collects "face sheet" data on the informants can explore if, and/or how, any particular phenomenon may be differentially distributed by gender, race, social class, age, and so forth. Whether, and to what extent, any phenomenon is generic is an empirical question that must be addressed anew for every new research topic.

Problems in Framing and Delivering the Instructions

Most of the instructions reviewed in Chapter 2, such as anonymity, going about one's daily life naturally, being nonjudgmental, and doing a timely write-up, are designed to maximize validity and minimize errors and biases. Nevertheless, there are methodological concerns connected with instructing informants to self-observe a predetermined activity. Informants report surprise at how often they experience the targeted phenomenon. Their new mindfulness means that they are experiencing their world differently. This raises the question of "reactivity"—whether the very act of doing instructed self-observation may change the way informants naturally operate in the world, altering the naturalness of the data.

Researchers who use informants—whether as questionnaire respondents, as interviewees, or as Systematic Self-Observation research adjuncts—must be concerned about reactivity bias. Just as a questionnaire item can create an opinion (as opposed to just measuring an existing one), asking informants to observe a phenomenon may influence them to produce, or alter, the phenomenon to be observed.

Is instructed self-observation intrinsically, or only potentially, reactive? The semantic difference between *self-awareness* and *self-consciousness* suggests that self-observation need not be reactive. To be "self-aware" means to observe self without judgment or tension, whereas "self-consciousness" entails a judgmental stance that alters behavior from its natural manner. Informants commonly report that their self-observing did not affect their behavior, but we have no way of knowing if the SSO instructions resulted in self-conscious behavior.

The type of examples given can influence subsequent observations. In our research, we gave two different classes the assignment to report instances of "pretending not to see." The generic features of the topic were discussed in both classes, but in one class we used examples of pretending that one does not see a person. The second class was given examples of pretending not to see a flaw (an unzipped zipper, food visibly stuck between teeth, a button that has come undone). Though each class reported instances of many types of "not seeing," each class gave significantly more instances of the type of examples the researcher had provided.

To mitigate this example bias, the researcher can give *no* examples at all, letting the informants produce their own sense of the topic. Or the researcher can give many and diverse examples, which may promote the perception of a broader field of phenomena for observation by the typical informant. Telling informants to include questionable instances will increase the range of observations and possibly contribute to the definition of the phenomenon.

Framing and delivering instructions are inherently biasing. Researchers may want to do preliminary studies of the impacts of variations in language or other variables, like the experiment using different examples described above. Researchers should strive to frame the instructions to reduce reactivity.

Problems in Observing the Phenomenon

Informants are told to observe *every* time the designated topic naturally occurs, but our discussions with the informants and examination of the data suggest that informants may be missing instances and/or details of the phenomenon. An imponderable feature of Systematic Self-Observation data is that it is difficult to know how much of an activity is unknowingly missed.

We usually give informants a set period of time during which they are to monitor every experience of the targeted phenomenon. But because the self-observation assignment occurs in the consuming and unrelenting flow of everyday life, informants report falling in and out of the kind of self-monitoring that is assigned. Sometimes they simply forget to do the assignment. Even informants with a high level of motivation report that they occasionally forget to be mindful and self-aware. In trying to recall and reconstruct the periods of forgetfulness, informants sometimes cannot recollect whether they have engaged in the activity being studied. If these lapses methodically exclude certain types of phenomena, they will be biasing the data.

Biases caused by the psychological and social dynamics particular to the topic can also jeopardize data quality. For example, self-concept and impression management issues, self-promotion motives, or the desire to accommodate, bluff, or please oneself or the researcher may contaminate the data by influencing what the informant would otherwise experience and/or report.

Systematic distortions of the data could also result from unknown features of the historical and social context of the informants' experiences. Sensitive topics may diminish the reliability of the self-observing informant. For example, in our study of lies, the kind of lies that create and perpetuate an aggrandized identity are rarely reported. Such lies may be too painful to observe and/or report. By contrast, the data abound with lies that were told to be polite or to avoid hurting another's feelings: that is, what are commonly referred to as "polite" or "white" lies.

The informants' general comments about their experiences were very encouraging. They said that doing SSO "didn't change anything" and that they felt that everything they observed was "natural." Because informants' self-observing skills can improve with practice, better trained and more experienced informants are likely to minimize periods of inattention, selectivity, and otherwise enhance the reliability and accuracy of SSO studies.

Problems in Recalling and
Reporting the Phenomenon

The instructions to accurately remember the phenomenon and to produce field notes raise perplexing methodological challenges. Much is unknown about the errors and biases involved in recall and reconstruction, and the nature of these problems will shift depending on the topic under study.

The challenge of recalling and reporting what was observed can be appreciated by considering the children's game "Telephone." In this game, each child has to secretly repeat to the next child what she or he just heard, illustrating the difficulty of simply capturing and reconstructing talk that has just been experienced. Students of conversational interaction know the incapacity of individuals to reconstruct the specifics of a verbal interaction (Psathas, 1995). Tape recorders can correct this source of error. Field notes of conversations lack the details (like vocalizations, silences, and overlapping talk) that appear in the technical transcripts of recorded interactions used by conversation analysts.

But taped and transcribed data cannot capture the participants' perceptions, motives, withheld actions, thoughts, and emotions, and these hidden features may be embellished or revised in the written version. Ideally, Systematic Self-Observation field notes are informants' best depictions of what actually occurred. Only the interpretations, analyses, motives, feelings, and impressions that occurred *at the time of the action* should be included—and *not* informants' *later* interpretations, analyses, and impressions of the actions as they write up their field notes. The extent to which informants respect this distinction is unknown. The best the researcher can do is to admonish informants not to introduce afterthoughts into their reports.

Chapter 2 showed how to design the instructions to encourage informant honesty and discourage errors or the falsification of the field notes. The actual impact of these instructions is unknown. In practice, all collected reports are assumed to be sincere and honest—but this is a dubious assumption. Some informants are more sensitive, more self-aware, or better writers. Some informants take the assignment more seriously than others. The quality of a set of reports can be very mixed.

Practical considerations can influence the accuracy of SSO data. All reports are supposed to be written immediately after the event. This may be impractical. The memory of the details of the event will diminish with time. Informants acknowledge that when they had to wait before writing up their observations, their field notes tended to be an impressionistic recollection. But both the stale, impressionistic recollections and the fresh observations that are recorded immediately are combined in any SSO data set.

A review of all our field reports also suggests that long and elaborate occurrences are less likely to be reported, at least in their full context. For example, lies and secrets are often embedded in long story formats. Similarly, a self-other comparison can be part of a long, complicated daydream. In these instances, greater recall and reconstruction demands are placed on the informant. The suspicious scarcity of reports that contain long stories or daydreams suggests a bias against reporting such cumbersome phenomena.

SSO studies of internal phenomena such as thoughts and emotions present their own special problems. Little is known about the accuracy of reconstruction—from memory—of thoughts and feelings. The written reconstructions of thoughts, like all translations, undoubtedly result in alterations, but the alterations occur in unknown ways. To capture and represent thoughts in words requires a translation because thoughts and words are not the same. Feelings and the words used to convey them are also not the same. The ways they differ and the ways the translations are achieved are unclear and unknown.

Finally, the field notes generated from SSO studies are like snapshots of an ongoing process. These snapshots may miss significant contextual, historical, and biographical details of these actions. For example, people do not talk to their children in the same way that they talk to their children's friends, to their peers at work, or to their boss. If unknown social, historical, or other contextual issues happen to be significant to the topic, a bias may distort the data.

The impact of the various methodological challenges depends on the abilities of the individual informant. The ability to self-observe and report is a skill that can be cultivated. Like all skills, it is differentially distributed. Unknown variations among informants in sensitivity, reflexive self-awareness, memory, and the ability to accurately reconstruct thoughts and dialogue make for great variability in the field notes. Variability would be a greater problem for an analysis that attempted to explicate the entire data set or the entire phenomenon. The confounding impact of these differences in the quality of the reports can be partially mitigated by selecting to analyze one or two features of the data and using sensitive instances to illustrate the analysis.

To deal with these problems, a judicious researcher should take the SSO data for nothing more than what they are: observations that have been perceived, recalled, and written up by informants. Some biases can be mitigated by limiting the analysis to the types of instances that the method is able to access rather than claiming to encompass the whole range of a phenomenon. SSO studies fit the interpretive mode and the "context of discovery" that typifies qualitative research, in which selected field reports are used as examples of the patterns that are revealed in the larger data set. The data can thus be used to illustrate inductively drawn generalizations.

Strengths of the Systematic Self-Observation Method

The methodological issues that characterize Systematic Self-Observation in general, and each particular SSO study, are often difficult to assess. But, with the exception of tape-recorded data, the same sorts of criticisms hold for almost every informant-based data-gathering method in the social sciences. Moreover, despite the methodological frailties of SSO, the method has demonstrated several strengths and promising features.

Every science needs the development of empirically based descriptions of its subject matter. SSO yields descriptions of social phenomena that cannot be accessed by the conventional methods of observation and interrogation. In fact, SSO, or some variant of SSO, seems to be the only way of gathering methodical data on the tacit, hidden, and elusive domain of social life.

Our research significantly allays the concern that SSO will alter the natural flow of the social and/or the cognitive and emotional phenomena observed.

Informants testify that the natural flow of everyday social life is unaltered. They report that their everyday social interactions and mental processes are so routinized and habituated, and possess so much inertia, that the awareness required for observing and reporting these activities does not seem to disturb their natural flow. The activities they observe thus are neither elicited nor derailed by the new attention they receive because they occur in social occasions that have their own inception, course, direction, and momentum.

Our SSO studies have demonstrated impressive reliability in the many replications of the studies that year after year have yielded strikingly consistent results. In study after study, the same phenomena appear in field notes as the same analytic stencils outline their forms. Even some of the quantitative measurements remain consistent. For example, in our repeated studies of self-other comparisons, the proportion of individuals seeing others as better off to individuals seeing themselves as better off is consistently about 2 to 1.

An important advantage of SSO over conventional ethnographic studies is that, with other methods, the worldview of the individual gathering the data is a filter that distorts the cultural or psychological world that is being studied. By contrast, the worldview (the perceptions, reactions, meanings, intentions, language, and emotions, etc.) of the SSO informant *is* the subject matter that is being studied. SSO captures the details of participating informants' activities in their own words. Thus, the researcher's theoretical formulations are not as blatantly imposed on the data as they are in conventional observation studies, in questionnaires, and in other researcher-prepared formats of data collection.

Another practical strength is that SSO studies are economical in terms of time and money. SSO is an especially practical research activity for teachers.

Despite the methodological questions surrounding SSO, the method has generated data that yield rich insights. SSO studies have provided new and nonintuitive information on a range of heretofore neglected topics, yielding theoretical gains that would be unimaginable without the empirical data generated by some form of SSO. The next chapter reviews a few of these SSO studies.

4. FOUR STUDIES GENERATED WITH SYSTEMATIC SELF-OBSERVATION

In this chapter, we review four of our own Systematic Self-Observation (SSO) studies—on telling *lies* (Rodriguez & Ryave, 1990), telling and receiving *secrets* (Rodriguez & Ryave, 1992), *withholding compliments* (Rodriguez, Ryave, & Tracewell, 1998), and feeling *envy* in self-other comparisons (Rodriguez & Ryave, 1998). The data were generated following the principles of SSO as detailed in Chapter 2. These data proved essential for developing nonintuitive insights and understandings of these relatively neglected topics. We present brief synopses of our findings and analyses.

SSO is a generic method that can be used by researchers with diverse orientations. Our analyses have been informed primarily by the work of Harvey Sacks, Erving Goffman, symbolic interactionism, ethnomethodology, semiotics, and conversation analysis. They represent just one of many ways that the data can be interrogated. These analyses show that it is possible to describe the details and underlying order of mundane social experiences that occur anywhere, with anyone, at any time.

Given the exploratory nature of the research and the qualitative nature of our data, we make little effort to try to produce a quantitative description of the phenomena. Instead, we employ the data in the context of discovery, where they serve as the basis for developing inductive analyses. In this research context, we use selected instances to illustrate our analyses.

Case Study 1:
Telling Lies in Everyday Life

Telling lies is conventionally a reproachable activity that is nevertheless a recurrent feature of social life. To explore this social anomaly, we put aside the moral issues to study lying as an expression of the organizational features of social interaction. We discovered that many of the lies self-observed by our informants were due to a sequential preference in language that ritualistically organizes social interactions and advances social solidarity (Goffman, 1967, p. 11; Heritage, 1984).

FINDING AN ANALYTIC FOCUS

Several recurrent themes and general observations emerged from our study. Despite the initial protestations of a few students that they "didn't tell lies," eventually all the informants observed themselves telling lies. The informants reported being surprised at how often they told lies in their everyday interactions. Only a minority of the lies reported were formulated in advance of some anticipated interaction. The vast majority were told on the spot, in the unrehearsed process of an unfolding interaction. Virtually all the informants reported that their spontaneous lies were easy to produce without changing the routine timing and pacing of interactions. We were surprised at the homogeneity of the data: The content, situations, and motivations of our informants' lies looked very similar.

Our observations that all the informants lied, that the vast majority of reported lies occurred spontaneously, and that those lies closely resembled one another suggest that lying emerges from the general features of social interaction. In other words, lying is not so much a matter of personality, social background, or moral predisposition; rather, the options available in conversation may present a normative framework in which lying is not only a possible action but a preferred one (Sacks, 1975).

LIES, INTERACTION SEQUENCES, AND RESPONSE PREFERENCES

In our study, most lies occurred when people made offers, invitations, compliments, requests, assessments, and complaints and when there was a demand for an acceptance or rejection of what was offered, requested, or stated. The preponderance of lies occurred in the response portion of these paired conversational activities.

Earlier research on conversation has demonstrated that there is a general systematic preference for acceptances over rejections (Pomerantz, 1978; Sacks, 1987). Acceptances are expressed directly and succinctly and occur with greater frequency than rejections. Rejections are avoided and, when expressed, tend to be delayed, muted, and camouflaged (Atkinson & Heritage, 1984, pp. 53-56). The informants' preference for acceptances over rejections apparently motivated many of the lies in our data.

For example, when the informants did not want to accept another's invitation or assessment, they fulfilled the preference for acceptance by lying. Consider the following two instances:

First Instance
Place: In a parking lot outside a high school.
Who: Basketball friend and myself.
Situation: Standing by our cars talking about nothing.

Friend: We play tomorrow in Pacific Palisades. Why don't you come see us play?
Me: Oh really? What time do you play?
Friend: We play at 7:30 on Friday. You should come down if you get a chance.
Me: Okay, I'll be there. [Lie]

Second Instance
Place: At home.
Who: Husband and myself.
Situation: During sex.

Husband: Good?
Me: Mmmm . . . mmm. [Lie]

The data are also replete with instances where an informant lies in accepting an offer, invitation, or request, only to later produce an additional lie to undo the initial acceptance and the obligation that it involved. The following instance illustrates this pattern:

Place: Two conversations. The first at school. The second one at home.
Who: Friend and myself, then mother and myself.
Situation: My friend wanted me to go to the movie with her. I was tired and didn't want to go but agreed.

Friend: How about going to the movies this evening. I'm dying to see *Gandhi*.
Me: Sounds good. [LIE] What time do you want to leave?
Friend: I'm not sure. As soon as I get home, I'll give you a call and we'll decide then.
Me: Okay.
(One hour and fifteen minutes later, at home, phone rings)
Me: Mom, will you get that, and if it's Janet, tell her I wasn't feeling well and went to bed. [LIE. I felt fine.]

A lie that minimizes or negates a rejection is a special case of the preference for acceptance. Rejections tend to be expressed indirectly and in a hesitant manner that minimizes, or even negates, their occurrence. Unlike expressions of acceptances, which are succinct and right to the point, the work of minimizing a rejection involves relatively extensive talk. In our data, many lies had the character of turning a rejection into an unfulfillable acceptance:

Place: Telephone conversation at home.
Who: Neighbor and me.
Situation: I received an invitation to a party which I did not really want to attend. There was an RSVP on it, so I had to respond. Finally, I called her at dinnertime, because I hoped she would be busy and would not have much time to talk.

Me: Thank you for the invitation, we would love to go but we already have a previous commitment, a business engagement. [Lie]

RITUAL LIES THAT AMELIORATE REJECTION

The same pattern of lying has been found in the structure of preinvitations, preoffers, prerequests, and so forth (Schegloff, 1980). Our informants anticipated needing/wanting to tell a lie to avoid rejecting a request, offer, invitation, or assessment. In the following conversation, the informant lies to avoid an outright rejection:

Place: Home.
Who: Phone conversation with my brother, who called.
Situation: My brother phoned me late Thursday. He often calls me for favors, especially on Friday, which is my day off.

Brother: What are your plans for Friday?
Me: I have an appointment with the dentist. [Lie]
Brother: I was going to ask you for a little favor, but since you're busy, I won't.

A DEVIANT CASE CLINCHES THE ANALYSIS

The following instance represents a deviation from the preference for acceptance. Here the informant lies to forthrightly *reject* the other's assessment:

Place: Having lunch at a restaurant.
Who: A friend and myself.
Situation: Spending an afternoon with a close friend.
Friend: I really don't care for my clothes, and I don't like the way my hair is done.
Me: I don't agree. You have nice taste [Lie] and your hair is refreshing. [Lie]
Friend: I don't know.
Me: Really! [Lie]

Until we reviewed this datum, the lies we found were always situated in acceptances, but here the lie is embedded in a direct and succinct rejection of another's assessment. However, it is a special case in that the lie is spoken in response to a self-deprecating assessment. Rejecting another's self-deprecation maintains their face and supports affiliation.

All the previous instances of lies led not just to acceptance of the other's statement, request, offer, or invitation but to support, sociability, or bonding. Thus, the preference for interactions that promote solidarity motivates many of the lies that are told in everyday life. In other words, in most instances, our informants lied to maintain affiliation.

Case Study 2: The Micropolitics
of the Secrets Told in Everyday Life

The act of telling someone a secret identifies her or him as special and contrives to strengthen the relationship by creating greater trust, greater intimacy, and a preference for being agreeable and accepting of the orientation of the secret teller. Sharing a secret thus invokes a micropolitical coalition. The large majority of the secrets in our data display a pattern that Sacks (1970a) referred to as an "overall structural organization." This structure includes (a) the secret frame (that announces the secret), (b) the receiver's acceptance or rejection of the obligations inherent in the secret frame, (c) the secret information, and (d) the response to the secret. Our analysis focuses on the activities that precede and follow the presentation of the secret.

FRAMING INFORMATION AS A SECRET

The information in most of the explicit secrets that were reported would not automatically identify them as secrets. Our data support the observations of Simmel (1950) and Bellman (1984) that there is nothing intrinsic to the content of transmitted information that necessarily constitutes it as a secret. It needs to be labeled as such by the teller and/or receiver, which then infuses the information with exclusivity, confidentiality, and the social implications of the structural form of "a secret."

The talk that introduces and identifies the secret is the "frame." The secret frame tends to inform the secret recipient that she or he has been especially selected. The frame also tends to set up the instructions and obligations regarding the transferability of the information. Below are a variety of typical secret frames:

First Secret Frame
Rachel: I'm so upset, I need to talk to someone but I'm afraid that someone we
know might hear about this. I really don't want *anyone* to know about it.

Second Secret Frame
B: I have news for you but you can't tell anyone. Especially, Lisa. Don't
tell her I told. Act surprised when she tells you. O.k.?

Third Secret Frame
A: Hello.
B: Hello Jean, this is Donna.
A: Oh, hi!

B: → I have something important to tell you, but you can't mention this to anyone at BIS.

In each instance, the secret giver specifies some population to be excluded from the information and seeks the recipient's willingness to abide by the exclusivity rule as a part of the offer. This frames the to-be-presented information as a secret. The secret frame takes the form of an implicit or explicit *contract*: "I will tell you—if you promise not to tell."

There is variability in how the excluded population is identified. A common practice is to exclude "anyone." Bellman (1984) noted that the use of *anyone* is metacommunicative. It is not to be construed to refer to an entire population; rather, the reference is really to some specifiable group of persons (Sacks, 1975).

The second secret frame begins by excluding "anyone" but soon specifies "Lisa." Curiously, the secret is information that Lisa already knows. In this example, it is transparent that the creation of a coalition with the recipient is more important than the transmission/nontransmission of information, since Lisa is expected to share the information later.

THE FORMULATION OF THE SECRET

Many of the secret frames in our data not only communicated that a secret was forthcoming but also "formulated" it by infusing the exclusive information with a particular meaning and significance. In the first secret frame above, the recipient is told that the information to be shared makes the teller "so upset." The third secret frame says the information is "something important." These formulations give the recipient the orientation from which to hear and respond to the concealed information. The speaker almost always ends the secret frame by giving the floor to the secret recipient before producing the secret information.

The secret frame serves several interactional functions: First, the secret giver alerts the recipient to avoid taking the floor until the information has been presented (Sacks, 1970b). Second, the formulation of the secret instructs the recipient on how to listen for, and recognize, the conclusion of the confidential information (Sacks, 1970b). A recipient can wait for the "upsetting news," for example, as a means for knowing *when* to respond and perhaps *how* to respond—"Boy, is that upsetting!" Finally, the preface permits the secret giver to take the floor in a manner that constrains the secret recipient to respond in terms of her or his willingness to accept (or reject) the secret contract.

RESPONDING TO THE SECRET FRAME

The secret frame is a "sequentially paired interaction" that demands an acceptance or rejection (Schegloff & Sacks, 1973). Our data convincingly support the general finding that there is an interactional preference for producing acceptances over rejections (Atkinson & Heritage, 1984, pp. 53-56). In *every* case in our data set, the secret recipient produced an immediate, succinct, and unequivocal acceptance. Below are three examples of this feature of the secret envelope (the acceptance is marked by →):

First Instance
B: I need to talk about this. Promise not to tell anyone.
A: →   I promise. What's up?

Second Instance
A: I want to tell you something about John, our boss, but don't mention it
       to anyone.
B: →   I won't say a word to a soul.

Third Instance
Chris: My history teacher is kind of "off the wall," but he gets the point across.
Me: I have a couple of teachers like that too. I can't hold this in any longer, I
       have to tell someone. Can I trust you?
Chris: → Go ahead you can trust me. What is it?

In these and many other instances, the secret recipient tended to echo the language and formulation introduced in the secret frame. The secret recipients regularly used the words and phrasing of the secret frame to build a parallel acceptance. Then, in each instance, the recipient returned the floor to hear the secret.

THE SECRET

Our study paid brief attention to the secrets themselves. Their understanding required historical and contextual knowledge that generally went beyond our data. We found that the reports of pregnancies, abortions, affairs, stigmas, misfortunes, indiscretions, and so forth, were quite uninteresting because the data were anonymous and thus all the tales were disconnected from people in our lives.

The secrets were strongly charged with political vectors. Words like *sad*, *disgusting*, and *awful* put a spin on the interpretation of the information.

Moreover, it is significant that the secrets were tales of misfortunes, indiscretions, limitations, and the flaws of others. Because they concerned some others' trouble, these tales painted the secret sharers in a better light than the unfortunate or stigmatized others. The implicit "us-them" stance regarding the unlucky or deviant others may contribute to the coalition-generating work of secret telling.

RESPONDING TO THE SECRET

Up to the point of telling the secret, the secret giver has been in a structurally dominant position. She or he has been in control of choosing to frame some information as a "secret," choosing the recipient, setting up the secret obligation, specifying the transferability rules, formulating the story, and conferring the information. But after the secret is told, this advantage is neutralized. Then the capacity to "show understanding" permits the secret recipient to act on the secret giver's definition of the situation by accepting or rejecting it. At this stage, the implicit bond and the building of a coalition can be affirmed or undermined.

As with the acceptance/rejection of the secret frame, there is a distinct preference for acceptance:

Place: Telephone conversation.
Who: Interaction between myself and a long-time friend.
Julie: You know Christopher is in Del Amigo, Psychological Hospital. I'm so upset because he needs alot of help and—oh! you just can't tell this to Steven.
Me: I won't, what's the matter?
Julie: Steven said that he is only going to let Christopher stay in the hospital two weeks because his insurance will run out then. It's so sad.
Me: → How sad, he needs to be there for six months to get the kind of help he needs.

Secret recipients frequently construct a parallel response by echoing the secret giver's formulations. Here, the statements "he needs alot of help" and "Steven said that he is only going to let Christopher stay in the hospital two weeks" are returned with "he needs to be there for six months . . ." The statement "It's so sad" is mimicked in "How sad . . ."

In showing understanding and acceptance of another's formulation of the situation, the recipient echoes the language used by the secret giver or changes the secret giver's words while keeping the same message: For example, "I'll meet you next week" becomes "Yes, next Thursday." An even stronger acceptance and bonding response is for the secret recipient to return new information (which may or may not be in the form of a secret) that adds to, or amplifies, the secret information and its formulation.

Outright rejection of the intended message of the secret is exceedingly rare. Rather, the recipient hints at rejection and disagreement by producing a downplayed acceptance or questioning the correctness of information. Consider the following hesitant acceptance (marked with →):

Place: In an automobile.
Who: My friend Debra and myself.
Situation: Debra wants to become pregnant but her live-in boyfriend, Dennis, does not want her to have a baby.

Debra: I want to have a baby but I can't allow Dennis to know about it—he doesn't want a child.

Me: How can you do that without his knowledge?

Debra: I'll let it happen and when I start to show, it'll be too late for him to object. Please don't tell anyone or even mention anything about it when you visit the house.

Me: → OK, if that's what you want, then it's OK with me, but I hope you know what you're doing.

Debra: I really want Dennis' baby.

Me: → Ok.

Usually secret telling works to create a close and positive bonding between the teller and the recipient. However, in the instance above, the recipient provides only the most tentative acceptance of the teller's intent (Glowacz, 1989), cautioning the teller with the phrase "I hope you know what you are doing." The final "Ok" is a minimal acceptance of the teller's intention. Though outright rejection is avoided, a full acceptance, with its commensurate impact of bonding and providing social support, is not given.

Our data set contained only one occasion where the recipient dramatically rejected the teller's negative characterization of a third party. The effect of rejecting the teller's formulation seriously negated the bonding of the secret construction and interaction. In terms of the coalition building, a choice was forced, and the recipient instead opted to align with the third party (who happened to be her/his sister).

DISCUSSION: THE MICROPOLITICS
OF SECRET-TELLING INTERACTIONS

Telling a secret establishes a bond between the participants and generates an asymmetry between them and some nonpresent third party(ies). However, on the level of the micropolitics of interaction, the secret, once told, also establishes a power asymmetry between the secret giver and the secret recipient. After a secret has been told, the secret teller is vulnerable to the secret receiver's judgment on several points. First, the secret teller may covertly characterize the teller as morally weak for having divulged the confidential information. What is more, the secret recipient now has the option of reporting to significant parties that the secret teller has divulged a confidence.

Second, the secret recipient has the choice of overtly accepting or rejecting the formulation (the social/political "spin") that the teller wants to give to the information. Furthermore, the recipient has the option of appearing to accept the formulation overtly while in actuality rejecting the formulation covertly (Rodriguez & Ryave, 1990).

The third postsecret vulnerability of the secret teller is that the secret recipient can overtly accept but covertly reject the coalition contrived by the secret sharing. Rejection of the bonding tends to be done covertly. For this reason, competent secret tellers carefully scrutinize the acceptances of the secret recipient to assess the political success of the secret coalition.

Muted or reticent acceptances of the secret information are worrisome because they may indicate a covert rejection of the formulation and/or coalition that the secret sharing proffered (Rodriguez & Ryave, 1990). By contrast, strong acceptances that echo the teller's formulation or, better yet, produce a parallel secret that makes the tellers and recipients equally vulnerable and on an equal footing are rewarding and indicate the success of the political dimension of the secret-sharing interaction.

It is probably because of the risks and vulnerabilities of secret telling that secret sharers sometimes experience postsecret disappointment and remorse— or the elation of successfully having pulled off a micropolitical *coup*.

Case Study 3: Withholding of Compliments and the Covert Management of Disaffiliation[5]

A compliment can readily enhance face and affiliation (Goffman, 1967; Wolfson & Manes, 1980). Thus, the decision to withhold a deserved compliment contrasts with participants' striving, in everyday interactions, for the promotion and maintenance of face and affiliation. Goffman (1967) argued that people not only defend their own face but also protect the face of others in the expectation that their face will be afforded the same protection (see also Holtgraves, 1992). Given the preference for affiliative actions (Heritage, 1984), we investigated why compliments aren't more common than they are and why individuals refrain from praising others.

Our Systematic Self-Observation research showed that informants sometimes consciously and intentionally chose not to deliver a compliment, and their reports readily explained why they withheld the praise. Two primary motivations for withholding a compliment emerged from the informants' reports: competitive situations and punitive sentiments.

MANAGING COMPETITIVE
CIRCUMSTANCES TO PRESERVE FACE

A compliment is frequently withheld when the informant perceives that the compliment will threaten or injure her or his own or some other's face or sense of self. The informants relate in their field notes that they are responding to the competitive features of social comparisons, where one individual's achievement implicates someone else's comparative failing.

A compliment to one party can injure or threaten the face and sense of self of another. The following instance, reported by one of the researchers, illustrates the inferential mechanisms by which withholding a deserved compliment can preserve and protect face:

> Situation: Teaching a class. Having finished a lesson, there was an opportunity for class participation/discussion. Numerous students offered opinions and/or questions. I was particularly impressed with the observations made by the fifth student to comment. I wanted to respond to this student's observations by praising their insightfulness. However, I withheld the praise I was feeling because I thought that it might make the other students who had previously commented feel bad—in comparison, which might undermine their morale. What praise I gave this exceptional student was minimal and did not contrast from the remarks I made to the other students.

This teacher's decision to withhold a compliment was informed by the awareness that the other students who spoke might hear the praise as an implicit criticism of their contribution, thus injuring their face. Sacks (1992) characterized compliments that inferentially provide a negative reflection on another party as "unsafe compliments" (pp. 461-466).

Our data contains only 3 instances of withholding a compliment because it is unsafe for the face of a third party, but almost 70 instances of withholding a compliment because it is unsafe for the face of the potential complimenter (the informant). In the following instance, saying something praiseworthy to the other might reveal the informant's comparatively diminished self with respect to the issue at hand and present a threat to her or his own face:

Place: At a friend's house.
Who: Friend and myself.
Occasion: My friend was showing me some papers that she had written and I thought they were very good but could not tell her because I think it was my jealousy that she had a better paper than I did.

When a hierarchical comparison is generated between comparable others, the basic ingredients of a character contest are in place (Goffman, 1967). In many of the informants' descriptions of instances where self and face were at stake, the language was rich with competitive and contest metaphors. For example:

Situation: Shooting pool in a bar with some friends from work. I'm getting my butt kicked for the third time in a row by my friend Stuart. He comes within two balls of running the table after breaking. It impressed the heck out of me, but I didn't say anything.
Reason: I realize that I am one lousy pool player, and this bums me out just a little. In order to appear indifferent to my inability to sink even the simplest shot, I pretend that I could care less about the whole game, and am unimpressed by someone who is better than me.

Self-diminishing comparisons and face-deflating emotions escort many of the instances of competitively inspired withholding of compliments. The relevance of comparable others, unsafe compliments, and the ongoing negotiation of face and social relations within a competitive context are all displayed in the instance below:

While working at my field placement, several interns were given an assignment to complete. . . . I stayed after work in order to do some research on the task. . . . I completed the assignment and also found additional information which would decrease the amount of work which people need to do. . . . Next day I turned in my assignment at 8:00 AM. (Note: The other interns did not turn in their assignment until 1:00 PM that day.)
Our supervisor told me, "You did a good job and thanks for finding this additional information, now we won't have to do as much work. If you keep this up, I will have to hire you after you graduate." The boss gave me this compli-

ment in front of the paid staff as well as the other interns. After giving the compliment, the paid staff came up to me and gave me compliments also. All the interns gave me a "dirty look" and walked away. During lunch break, in the lunch room, when one [of the] paid staff thanked me for cutting their work load down, the other interns quickly tried to get the person who was giving the compliment to change the subject.

Unlike the teacher in the earlier instance, the supervisor and other paid staff did not refrain from making an "unsafe compliment" before this informant's peers. The presumed comparative diminishment of the other interns gave the informant a reason why these peers withheld compliments.

PUNITIVE SENTIMENTS: REPORTS OF EARLIER NORM VIOLATIONS

Of the 351 instances collected, about one fourth reported that the informant consciously withheld a compliment as a reproof of some earlier misbehavior. In each of these cases, the informant assumed the deservedness of the compliment, but some unacceptable behavior or attitude of the potential complimentee disqualified her or him from receiving the praise. Ironically, the most commonly reported theme involved breaches of the informant's sense of the norms pertaining to compliment etiquette (Pomerantz, 1978).

Compliments, like sympathy, are a kind of social capital. Those who have not invested them in others in the past cannot count on a current return (Clark, 1987):

> I work with a fellow employee, named John. John will rarely compliment another co-worker when appropriate. . . . Recently, I was in a joint staff meeting that included John's presence. The manager informed the group about John's latest venture. The manager complimented John on his research on a vital project. A few members of the group joined in on the "back patting" and John was all smiles. I have sat in on many of these same types of meetings, and I had the pleasure of hearing the manager praise other co-workers, as well as me. At these meetings, I noticed John rarely, if ever, extended a "pat-on-the-back" to another person.
>
> With this memory in mind, when John was placed on center stage, I elected not to extend John a compliment. . . . John will need to change, or at least show some improvement. . . . I will continue to withhold any compliments directed toward John until he learns how to hold his co-workers in higher esteem.

Many informants give considerable attention to monitoring and remembering the other's past complimenting behaviors. Past failures to compliment engendered retaliatory sentiments in the informant that led to a withheld compliment.

The norm against self-praise is part of the demeanor that should be maintained regarding complimentable achievements (Pomerantz, 1978). Self-praise can bring forth a punitive sentiment that can undermine the offering of a compliment:

Place: Classroom.
Who: Fellow student and me.
Situation: Right before class begins, she walks in wearing a new outfit.

Student: Hi! How are you?

Me: Fine, thanks! How are you?

Student: I feel good, especially with my new outfit on, girl. It is fierce. I know I
        look good today.

Me: (I smile and kind of chuckle.) [True, she was wearing a nice outfit. But I
        withheld my compliment on it because I felt I didn't need her head to
        get any bigger.]

THE COVERT MANAGEMENT
OF DISAFFILIATIVE SENTIMENTS

What factors affect the visibility and the social accountability of an intended nonaction of consciously choosing to withhold a compliment? Withheld compliments fall on a continuum of social visibility from ritual complimentable situations to moments when withheld praise may be invisible because it is unrelated to the action at hand. The withholdings in compliment-relevant situations are more visible. The more formal and ritualized the complimentable situation, the more likely it is that a compliment will be expected and that its absence will be noticed. Many situational and interactional factors affect the degree of social visibility of a withheld compliment. In the following instance, nearly all present extend a round of compliments to an individual. The informant explains her/his nonaction in terms of the expanded ego rationale:

An employee at my job makes the majority of her clothing. She came today with an outfit on that I had never seen before. Everyone in the office was admiring the outfit, while I looked and walked the other way. I said nothing because she is already too conceited.

Cases of fishing for a compliment also make a withheld compliment especially visible:

> I had just gotten back a big research paper from last semester which I had worked extremely hard on. I received an "A" and was very pleased. I gave the paper to my boyfriend in hopes of a big "I'm proud of you" from him. He looked at it, set it down, and began to talk about his day at work. I was very hurt by this, he knew how hard I worked.

Although there are occasional situational and relational imperatives that make a withheld compliment noticeable, there are also factors that mask and protect it. A withheld compliment is hidden information that can only be suspected or inferred. Several factors serve to minimize accountability, but above all is the fact that *participants cannot know whether a nonaction is conscious and meaningful or just an unintended slip of social attention.*

In many interactions, the lack of a clear sequential imperative to compliment diminishes a withheld compliment's visibility. The looseness in conversational placement and timing of the compliments can sometimes lessen the noticeability of their nonproduction and the likelihood that the potential compliment giver will be called upon to explain or account for her or his nonaction. Actions that correct another's social behavior can be offensive and inappropriate (Schegloff, Jefferson, & Sacks, 1977). So the intended or unintended omission of praise is likely to go (overtly) unchallenged. Moreover, it is always possible that the compliment is still forthcoming.

Accountability is greatly diminished by the fact that challenging a withheld compliment violates the norm against self-praise (Pomerantz, 1978). Furthermore, challenging the withholding of a deserved compliment is a confrontational act that is dispreferred (Maynard, 1985).

The suspected withholding is uncontested even in those reports of more socially visible instances. In fact, there were *no* instances in our data where the withholding of a compliment was openly challenged. The fact that the withholder of praise is not likely to be overtly held accountable or to generate a visibly retaliatory reaction (at least not in the immediate interaction) are the factors that contribute to and define its opaque and covert character.

DISCUSSION: MANAGING DISAFFILIATIVENESS

Friends, spouses, siblings, cousins, roommates, fellow employees, and classmates populate the relationships reported in our data. Thus, the reports of disaffiliative acts of withholding merited social recognition from another occurred between people who were in ongoing relationships that required and typically contrived for affiliation. An apparent strain exists between the competitive situations and punitive sentiments reported in our data and the interactional preference for actions that promote and conserve social bonds.

How do individuals generally manage disaffiliative sentiments? There are a range of options on a continuum of expressiveness. At one extreme, these sentiments can be muffled and concealed completely. A second option is that a polite lie can be told such that disaffiliative sentiments surface as their opposite (Rodriguez & Ryave, 1990). Third, the sentiments can be expressed—but in confidence and to a safe third party (Bergmann, 1993; Rodriguez & Ryave, 1992, 1993). Fourth, they can be cautiously and obliquely manifested—but in a covert, muted, and downplayed manner. Finally, they can be directly and openly expressed in private or, with greater aggravation, in a public setting, establishing the ingredients for the creation of open conflict (e.g., Goodwin, 1982, 1983; Goodwin & Goodwin, 1990; Maynard, 1985; Rodriguez & Ryave, 1995). All the options except the last one, to different degrees, yield to the preference for affiliation and avoidance of conflict. On this continuum, the withholding of compliments fits the fourth option in that even if the nonaction of a withheld compliment is noticed, it is most likely to remain unaddressed in order to avoid violating the norms against self-praise and open confrontational challenges.

A wide range of studies of interaction document a multitude of ways in which people contrive for affiliation. By contrast, this study identified *a hostile undercurrent* that exists in many everyday interactions. The withholding of compliments is one covert manifestation of this disaffiliative undercurrent.

Case Study 4: Envy in the Social Comparisons of Everyday Life

Social psychologists have predominantly pursued the study of social comparisons using the traditional experimental and behavioral methods of the established social science paradigm (Festinger, 1954; Rosenberg, 1979; Suls & Wills, 1991). There have been few efforts to capture social comparisons as they naturally occur in everyday life (Wood, 1989). Furthermore, only a few studies have focused on envy or the other emotional consequences of social comparison (Salovey, 1991; Tessar, 1991). Our Systematic Self-Observation study explored the social comparison processes that generate envious feelings and identified some of the social consequences of envy.

THE THREE ESSENTIAL
FEATURES OF SOCIAL COMPARISON

Informants were asked to self-observe moments when they made self–other comparisons. The resulting data showed that three features constitute a social comparison. The first is the *value or trait*. Anything can serve as a basis for comparison, although traits like physique, weight, hair, personality, intelligence, cars, and happiness were commonly reported.

The second feature is the *comparable other*. Our data indicated that informants carefully chose whom they drew on to construct a social comparison. Not only did each party to the comparison have to possess the trait, but it was important that the other be perceived as a peer or "comparable other." The following instance demonstrates that the comparability of the other can be readily canceled:

> I was working in a doctor's office at Kaiser the other day when I started looking at a very attractive lady wearing a straight sweater dress. She appeared to be about my age and height, but for some reason I kept watching her. When she stood up, everyone was looking at her; men and women were admiring her beautiful shape. I was comparing my shape with her until I heard her tell a lady sitting next to her that she works out at a gym several times during the week. I stopped comparing myself to her when I remembered that I can't exercise now because of my medical problems.

Here, someone who at first seemed to be a peer turns out not to be a fair match; thus, she is no longer a comparable other, and the social comparison is discarded on the spot.

The third feature is the *comparative evaluation*. Every social comparison involves an evaluation that takes one of four basic forms: the same as, just different from, better than, or worse than the comparable other with regard to the trait or value.

A comparison in which the comparable other is lower than or inferior to the self is referred to as a "downward comparison" (Wood, 1989). One in which the comparable other ranks higher than or superior to the self is called an "upward comparison." The next two instances illustrate these two types:

> First Instance
> Situation: A female and I were talking; rather, I was listening. She was telling me how she was hardly surviving all the woes in her life. I found myself going off into comparison land and was deciding I had more woes than she had and I was doing a much better job getting through them. I don't think I like this assignment.

Second Instance

Situation: I was talking on the phone with a co-worker. During the conversation he reported, much to my surprise, that he recently received a raise. Although I congratulated him, I felt upset and jealous and wondered to myself why I also did not receive a raise. I felt unappreciated and questioned my worth. After the conversation, I spent much of the evening thinking about this.

In nonhierarchical comparisons, informants perceive themselves as being either "the same" or "different," as is demonstrated in the following two instances:

First Instance

Situation: In my Writing Adjunct Class, I was talking with one of my classmates about the same advisor we had for the previous semester. She was talking about how badly he has treated her and the way he talked down to her made her feel smaller than a pea. I responded that I felt the same way when he was advising me. I just wanted to crawl under a rock and die. It felt good that we both had the same experience.

Second Instance

Situation: The other day in my literature class something made me look around the room while the professor was lecturing. I noticed the majority of the class was recording on paper practically every word the professor had spoken. I felt I was the only one different, as I did more listening than writing.

Our data contained 1,486 instances of social comparison. The frequency of each type of comparative evaluation is reported in Table 4.1.

The table shows that the reported social comparisons produced in everyday life are overwhelmingly hierarchical. These have very different consequences than nonhierarchical comparisons for the relationships of the people involved. Equivalent social comparisons support solidarity and are bonding, whereas hierarchical comparisons are infused with competitiveness (Rodriguez & Ryave, 1993).

UPWARD SOCIAL COMPARISONS
AND THE CONDITIONS FOR ENVY

Envy can occur when someone constructs an upward social comparison in which she or he is not doing as well as the comparable other (Schoeck, 1969). The instructions for data collection did not ask the informants to record envy or any other emotional reactions. The 936 upward social comparisons ranged from cases with an absence of envy to ones strongly imbued with the sentiment.

TABLE 4.1 Frequency Distribution of Comparative Evaluations

Comparative Type	Frequency	%
I. Hierarchical		
Downward	516	34.7
Upward	936	63.0
II. Nonhierarchical		
Same	29	2.0
Different	5	0.3
Total	1,486	100.0

The upward social comparisons that engendered envy were characterized by three features. First, the comparer focused on the ways in which the comparable other's achievement/success diminished her or his own sense of self and/or face. Second, the degree of diminishment of self and/or face was influenced by how self-defining or relevant the trait was to the comparer. Finally, the degree to which envy was generated reflected the extent to which the comparable other was a peer and possible rival in terms of the trait. Contrasting the instances where any of these conditions of envy were absent to instances where they were all present showed the importance of these three conditions.

Although in every instance of an upward social comparison the comparer was not doing as well as the comparable other, the informant did not always experience a diminished sense of self. In several instances, the informant admired the positive achievements of the comparable other to fuel a desire for self-improvement. For example:

I was visiting my 37-year-old sister-in-law, who is a mother of two. She was getting ready to go out for the evening. I compared the way she was able to get ready and leave the house so quickly, when for me it is such a production. I admired her style and decided I too would try to be that organized.

This instance illustrates Festinger's (1954) view of the social comparison process as a source of information for self-improvement. In cases like this, the comparable other is experienced as a role model and inspiration.

Not all traits were equally important to our informants. There were a few upward social comparisons where the potential for envy was lessened because the comparer saw the comparable trait as not relevant:

> While talking with my neighbor the other day, admiring his gardening and landscaping, I realized how unhandy I was, particularly in the yard. I have a gardener who comes weekly. I have no idea of the names of plants and trees on my property, and flowers are nonexistent (except for the rose bushes that I have no idea how to prune). I should try to be more like my neighbor.

This report gives little indication of envy. It suggests that the trait (gardening skills) is not a preoccupation of the informant but is being considered only on the occasion of the interaction. The neighbor's gardening is admired and becomes a possible project.

The third variable in our study was the degree to which the comparable other was perceived as a peer and/or rival with respect to the trait. The greater the similarity in status, the greater competitive comparability and potential for envy. The following report illustrates how the invidious feature of an upward comparison can be weakened by undermining the similarity between the informant and the comparable other. As the similarity dissolves, the initial pangs of diminished self and envy evaporate:

> I met with the mother of my daughter's best friend this morning. I knew she did aerobics regularly and I've always thought she looked great. I found myself comparing my body to her this time. I actually started looking for flaws in her body in an effort to feel better about my own body. Then I began to feel ridiculous because we have very different body shapes. After realizing this, I felt proud of both of us for looking as good as we do at our age.

Reports infused with envy were common. In the following instance, the comparer focuses on how her self-image, private and/or public, is diminished and how the comparable others are peers/rivals with respect to a trait that is significant to the informant:

> Place: My work.
> Who: Myself and two coworkers.
> Situation: Nonverbal. I was looking at the other 2 employees. They are both very thin and petite, and always look great.
> Comparison: I felt "less than" them because they're thin and I'm overweight. I felt like they must have all the self-control in the world, while I have none.

Although admiration is expressed, the informant observes the good looks of these comparable others with attention to what she lacks and the comparable others possess.

Though many of the social comparisons may have had a historical context, the informants' field notes demonstrated that the overwhelming preponderance of the social comparisons occurring in everyday life are experienced in an on-the-spot, spontaneous, and emergent fashion. The social comparisons in our data were rarely anticipated or part of some conscious project, as they are often portrayed in the social comparison literature (Wood, 1989). Most reports in our data illustrated the unanticipated nature of these constructions.

In some cases, the upward comparison was so damaging to the self that hostile invidious sentiments were expressed in the notes:

> My friend is on a weight loss program and has lost ten pounds in the last two weeks and she was bragging to me about her accomplishment. Outwardly I was happy for her but inwardly I was saying to myself, "Why did she have to make me feel like a beached whale, while telling me how she feels about her weight loss." I hoped that she would put the weight back on and more.

The fact that 98% of all the reported social comparisons were hierarchical lends support for the idea that the informants had a competitive predisposition toward the comparable other. What is done with these emotions? How are they managed during social contact?

VERBALIZED VERSUS NONVERBALIZED SOCIAL COMPARISONS

The 34 nonhierarchical comparisons in our data were typically voiced as soon as they occurred. The "we're the same" comparisons were affiliative, and their expression enhanced the social bond. By contrast, the overwhelming preponderance of hierarchical social comparisons were not voiced.

If the downward social comparisons were voiced, they would be both bragging and a put-down. These are socially inappropriate and antagonistic actions that threaten the face of the comparable other (Goffman, 1967; Heritage, 1984). The 23 out of 516 instances of verbalized downward comparisons were almost exclusively delivered *to a third party*. In all but one case, the comparer and the third party agreed on the negative assessment of the comparable other. Because they were filled with agreement, these exchanges enhanced the social bond.

Very few upward comparisons were verbalized. The stigma associated with being seen as envious can be appreciated by the fact that there was not a single instance in the 936 reports of upward comparisons where an informant spelled out to the comparable other or even a third party that she or he was filled with envy. We term these suppressed experiences *"muted thoughts"*: *reactions that are not readily candidates for social expression.*

Informants had the option of ignoring the self-diminishing facet of an upward comparison and just complimenting the other person. After all, compliments between peers are affiliative (Goffman, 1967; Wolfson & Manes, 1980). Yet the data showed very few instances where a compliment was expressed. These upward comparisons were muted thoughts.

Praise was withheld even in the instances where the observer reported constructing an upward comparison filled with admiration for the comparable other. Among the handful of verbalized upward social comparisons in which a compliment was delivered, the observers were not generous with their praise. For example, in the following instance, a grudging tone was used because the compliment was constructed in a downplayed and backhanded manner:

> Place: At home.
> Who: Female friend and myself.
> Situation: Sitting at table visiting.
>
> Me: What, are you getting anorexia?
> Friend: No, why?
> Me: You've lost so much weight since the last time I saw you. I wish I could be as skinny. What a twig.

ENVY: A HIDDEN EMOTION

Our interrogation of the data leads us to observe that envious social comparisons occur regularly in everyday life but that they are carefully hidden. There are grounds for concealing envy: To be perceived as envious is to tacitly suggest a diminished sense of self that damages face (Sabini & Silver, 1982, p. 25). Envious emotions shift the relationship between self and other toward a competitive or antagonistic orientation that damages the affiliativeness of the social bond. Disapprobation of envy is universal.

Friends, spouses, siblings, cousins, roommates, fellow employees, and classmates are most frequently chosen as the comparable other. Competitively imbued hierarchical comparisons occur between participants who are in ongoing relationships that require affiliativeness (Heritage, 1984). These social comparisons are muted thoughts, and the envious emotions are masked. The maintenance of face and the normative order that contrives for the preference for affiliative actions (Brown & Levinson, 1987; Heritage, 1984), account for the concealing of envy. Nevertheless, our research suggests that competitiveness and envy remain a buzzing undercurrent in the dramas of everyday social life.

Analytic Insights Generated by These Systematic Self-Observation Studies

Every research method captures a unique perspective on the phenomena it studies. Because the Systematic Self-Observation data that we gathered for these studies reached for the personal and hidden actions, and because the informants knew that their reports would be anonymous, these studies are candid reports of particular features of people's covert social activities. The manipulativeness of lies, the micropolitics that underlie secret sharing, the competitive and punitive motives behind withheld compliments, and the competitiveness and envy embedded in underlying self-other comparisons all betray an undercurrent of selfish, manipulative, hostile, and antisocial feelings and motives fueling many social actions. This undercurrent has been expressed in literature and the arts, but because it exists in a tacit and covert domain, it has not been readily accessible for study.

Our research with SSO has disclosed and, in a small way, begun to describe phenomena that have received little prior study: the *muted thoughts* (including the hidden emotions and the tacit motives) of everyday life. These are the real observations, opinions, strategies, meanings, resentments, criticisms, complaints, feelings, motives, and so on, that underlie people's actions and/or attitudes but that *are not candidates for social expression*. Our data show that this underworld of muted thoughts and emotions occasionally finds expression to a third party. (In fact, complaining about and criticizing someone to a third party can be a bonding activity.) But some muted thoughts (like upward self-other comparisons with a peer) are so face diminishing that they are practically never voiced. These data show the existence of tacit motives that drive behaviors like telling lies.

The covert undercurrents of social behavior that these SSO studies have made available for researchers and theorists reveal a promising domain of human phenomena that calls out to be studied.

5. OTHER APPLICATIONS OF SYSTEMATIC SELF-OBSERVATION

The primary purpose of this monograph has been to describe and explain how to use Systematic Self-Observation (SSO) as a research method. SSO can also be used for social science pedagogy, for therapy, and for self-development. In this chapter, we take up these four applications, discussing suggested topics for future SSO research, SSO's use as a teaching tool, its potential applications as therapeutic tool, and its relation to practices associated with spiritual development.

Researchable Systematic Self-Observation Topics

The theoretical and practical issues that identify the appropriate realm of experience for research using Systematic Self-Observation are discussed in Chapters 1 and 2. The basic ideas for developing researchable topics are found in Weber's (1967) classic definition of the realm of social conduct: that is, subjective meanings and socially oriented, mental, or external actions or nonactions (p. 1). Subjective experiences, mental processes, nonactions, and other hidden aspects of social conduct define the most appropriate subject matter for future SSO research. The following suggestions for generating SSO topics demonstrate promising ways of approaching this elusive and taken-for-granted domain of social life.

Potential topics exist in the many mundane features and idiomatic sayings of everyday life, such as "regretting how something 'came out' [i.e., was said]," "making a fool of yourself," "being at a loss for words," "name dropping," "disclosing oneself," "walking away," "overhearing," "bad manners," "not caring," "fishing for compliments," "gossiping," "complaining," "keeping mum," "stuffing it," "not knowing how to say something," "feeling remorse over something said/unsaid," "making/not making [eye/telephone] contact," "acting dumb," "buttering someone up," "being self-conscious," "feeling unfairly treated," "feeling embarrassed," "being insulted/insulting," "feeling sad/glad over another's failure/success," "wishing others well/harm," "losing it," "refraining from [bragging/bothering/blaming, etc.]," "not noticing [flaws, someone, hostility, bad manners, instructions, directions, a put-down, etc.]," "being taken/not taken [seriously/for granted]," "kissing up," and so on.

Emotions, sentiments, or psychological states can be researched. Informants can look for instances in which they experience shame, anger, fear, joy, anticipation, hopelessness, distrust, retaliation, helplessness, confusion, compassion, enthusiasm, envy, and so on. These studies can begin to identify where these sentiments and emotions are located in people's lives.

The situated manifestation of thoughts and feelings that relate to self and the attitudes and beliefs that they reveal are a gold mine for researchers. They include such topics as "self-blame," "self-congratulations," "self-confidence," "self-defensiveness" "self-distrusting," "self-sacrificing," "self-sufficiency," "selflessness," and "self-hatred." Similarly, particular thoughts and emotions that relate to another person or to a group can be selected for study.

A single, general topic can be narrowed and focused into several separate topics for study. For example, "criticizing" can be studied as "*withholding* criticism," "*receiving* criticism," "*reliving* criticism," "*emotions, thoughts, or motives* when criticizing or receiving criticism," "criticisms *delivered to a third party*," "*fearing* criticism," and so on. Many other topics can be similarly approached by using these same analytic templates: for example, "insulting," "gossiping," "envying," "flirting," "blaming," "pressuring," "ridiculing," "sympathizing," "bragging," and "overlooking [some behavior/flaw]."

The *antitheses* of topics (like the opposite of criticism: praise) can also be mined for SSO topics. Broad concepts like shame and pride are best focused into more specified topics, such as "shame (or pride) over [looks, possessions, affiliation, performance, ethnic/racial identity, etc.]," "suspected feelings of shame (or pride)," and "faking shame (or pride)." Some other generic antithetical phenomena include feeling "superior (or inferior)," "being included (or excluded) [in information, invitation, conversation, etc.]," "being open (or being secretive) [about feelings, information, thoughts, etc.]," "being ignorant (or knowledgeable) [about anything]," "anticipating (dreading) [some focus]," "being at an advantage (at a disadvantage)," "being in control (out of control)," "being patient (impatient)," "feeling appropriate (inappropriate)," and "feeling confident (unsure)."

The possibility of *inauthentic* as well as sincere actions and the possibility of *dissembling activities* suggest other ways of focusing. Topics like showing "surprise," "affection," "praise," "sympathy," "modesty," "concern," "love," "fear," "interest," and "generosity" can be changed into their insincere forms: "faking surprise," "hiding surprise," "portraying false affection," "hiding one's affection," "producing insincere compliments," "displaying false modesty," "faking sympathy" (and "faking lack of sympathy"), "acting worried" (and "acting unworried"), "acting concerned" (and "acting unconcerned"), "acting happy" (and "acting unhappy"), "acting interested" (and "acting uninterested"), "showing false generosity," and so on.

Inauthentic and dissembled actions like "faking surprise" and "hiding surprise" can also be expanded to *suspected* fake or hidden actions like "suspected fake surprise" or "suspected hidden surprise." We were able to combine the assignment of observing one's own actions with observing one's suspicions of their occurrence in others in a few of our studies. In our research on withheld compliments, the informants observed themselves withholding compliments as well as instances when they suspected that a deserved compliment was being withheld from them.

These common actions, nonactions, thoughts, feelings, and motives and another hundred variations of them can be drawn on for topics by being narrowed down into phenomena that are more or less single, focused, intermittent, bounded, of short duration, and described in the vernacular. Researchers can also explore deviating from these parameters to develop variant SSO studies.

Researchers can also partially or totally discard anonymity and get "face sheet" data on class, gender, age, race, ethnicity, and so on to explore how informants in these subgroups may differ in their expression of the phenomenon. For example, do women and men tell lies differently? Do older informants express or withhold complaints or compliments differently than younger ones?

Researchers exploring how covert phenomena like thoughts, meanings, motives, and emotions are socially located can use some variant of SSO to explore their subject. For example, conversation analysts can do SSO studies of selected emotions, motives, thoughts, meanings, and so forth, that the interactant-informants may be experiencing in any given setting, in combination with taped data.

Researchers can even use SSO in the arena of experimental studies by asking informants to systematically self-observe some feature of their inner life while participating in an experiment. Researchers of different theoretical persuasions studying interaction, settings, or psychological experiences can use SSO to reveal the thoughts and emotions of the participants in any setting.

Psychotherapy processes and outcomes can both be studied using SSO. A form of SSO is already used by behaviorist researchers who have clients keep track of how and why their symptoms emerge. The therapist and client can also identify the issue to be worked on and have the client use SSO to keep track of how and when it manifested itself in her or his life (A. Bohart, personal communication, May 22, 2001).

Finally, the SSO method itself identifies another set of possible research studies: The perplexing methodological issues of noticing, recalling, and reporting reviewed in Chapter 3 suggest research projects.

The possibilities for research are as broad as the researcher's insights into the blatant or nuanced features of intrapersonal and interpersonal life. We enthusiastically anticipate the development of the research on daily social life to which SSO is so suited, as well as the many other variants of SSO research that wait to be developed.

Systematic Self-Observation
as Pedagogy

Systematic Self-Observation is useful in the classroom. The teacher-student relationship is congruent and compatible with the researcher-informant roles. Students are especially good informants because they tend to be intelligent and literate and can readily learn to sensitively observe their own experiences. Doing SSO research with our college classes has contributed to students' education in the social sciences.

The detailed instructions for developing a SSO research study were provided in Chapter 2. A few training exercises should be given, perhaps using replications of existing studies; then the students are ready to start watching for the new research topic and writing up their observations. The admonitions to be sensitive and conscientious observers are bolstered by their awareness that they are doing real research where *they* are in control of the quality of the data.

The data-gathering process is only half of the teaching experience with SSO. After submitting her or his anonymous field notes, each informant receives a compilation of the whole class's (anonymous) data set. This data set becomes the basis for class discussions and an assignment to produce an analysis of some aspect of the data.

We have made participation in our studies optional and anonymous, yet it is unusual for a student not to at least try to participate in the data-gathering phase of our studies. The students frequently become enthusiastic informants because the topics have been familiar and interesting to them. They get especially engaged in the spirit of the research after they review their class's (anonymous) data set and see that others' experiences and behaviors are very much like their own.

Students are told to write up a careful data-centered analysis of something (or some things) they see going on in one, two, a few, or all of the instances. They are instructed to "stay close to the data" rather than making broad generalizations or moral judgments about society or human nature. They are told to work with one or a few instances at a time to see if they can find "a pattern or an organizing logic" in the data set or one feature of it.

Many budding theorists relish this challenge. Students learn to construct a data-oriented inductive analysis. Their interest and motivation to be even more sensitive informants grows in subsequent research projects. They become very interested in hearing their professor's analysis. The social science project of describing and understanding everyday human experiences comes to life for our students.

Many discussions of the various principles of the scientific method emerge naturally from the process of preparing the students to be effective informants and data analysts. These class assignments ask them to deal directly and concretely with core issues of social science, such as the centrality of empirical evidence, analysis, conceptualization, sampling, theory building, induction, validity, reliability, error, bias, reactivity, deviant case analysis, and replication.

Getting students involved in the full cycle of a study demystifies and democratizes the research process. Our students tell us directly, and in their anonymous course evaluations, that the SSO studies have been an excellent learning experience for them.

Using Systematic
Self-Observation for Therapy

The informants in our Systematic Self-Observation research projects report a growing awareness of their own personal experiences of the phenomena we study. They learn to see their own patterns as well as the common grounds and dynamics of others' behaviors. The simple act of noticing, of observing one's own behavior—of finally "seeing" some feature of personal experience without judgment—produces the objectivity and insight that can lead to self-change. The possible therapeutic value of SSO is suggested by the growth that informants experience in reflexively self-observing, in writing up their experiences, and in participating in classroom exercises where they review the whole data set and "see themselves" in the reports of others.

We couch the proposed use of SSO as an adjunct to therapy with the disclaimer that it is speculative. We have no experience with SSO as a therapeutic tool. The objectives of therapy are very different from those of a research method. Therapy is about healing something that is troubling. What we have seen is that SSO improves self-awareness and expands the informant's understanding of self and of others. The insight that others are similar is reassuring and comforting, and it leads to greater compassion and empathy. These features of SSO are what lead us to speculate on the potential uses of SSO as a therapeutic practice.

Could group therapy using SSO on a common problem contribute to the healing of participants? Could SSO work for one-on-one therapy? Five features of the SSO process recommend it for therapy.

First, just naming and bringing the troubling topic out into the open to a group or a therapist, where it can be discussed, is a necessary step in making a change. Weight Watchers, Alcoholics Anonymous, and a variety of group therapies demonstrate that social sharing is therapeutic. Second, the psychological task of systematically self-observing—without judging, interrupting, speeding up, slowing down, or in any way changing the phenomenon—accesses the roots of the trouble in the tacit dimension. Simply noticing the phenomenon when it pops up in one's everyday life is a feat of self-mastery.

SSO can cut through the hidden and tacit levels of the troublesome phenomenon so that its antecedents can be identified. We speculate that doing an SSO research on one's own personal antecedents and triggers (like feeling tension in one's jaw for those who experience attacks of violent rage or having a certain self-deprecating memory or thought for the depressed) could lead to using these as a "warning system" to alert the subject to take actions to derail the upcoming trouble. For example, in anger management therapies, individuals are taught to self-observe for the particular symptoms that they exhibit just before rage leads them into violent behavior (Pence & Paymar, 1986). By learning to notice these signals of their mounting anger, they are able to take a "time-out" to cool down.

Third, the nonjudgmental, objective SSO write-up immediately following an instance can be therapeutic. The write-up itself is an engaging form of "time-out." Keeping a journal has been shown to be therapeutic (Progoff, 1975). The individual does the write-up with the imagined audience of her or his therapist or the group when she or he has just finished facing the trouble and is in most need of support.

The fourth therapeutic potential of SSO lies in the act of submitting the data to the therapist or the group. The admonition to suspend making judgments may be of special importance. Turning in one's self-observations is a public "owning up," yet with either anonymity or confidentiality rules in place, it can be a safe confession.

Finally, SSO may be especially suited to group work because sharing experiences, in writing as well as face to face, with others who have the same problems may amplify the dynamic magic of group therapy. Moreover, the others' written reports will probably look so familiar that it will sound just like the participant's own experiences. Thus, participants will no longer be alone with their problems (Rose & LeCroy, 1991). If their guilt and shame are diminished, they can face their trouble with greater self-acceptance and a sense of challenge. Others are experiencing the world much as they do. Others suffer just like they do. Their perception of their personal trouble is put into the larger perspective of others who are facing the same struggle. Their individual challenge is amplified by being part of their group's mission.

Self-Observation and
Self/Spiritual Development Practices

The moral and ethical concerns over the impact of Systematic Self-Observation on informants, discussed earlier in Chapter 2, led to the proposal that SSO might actually be beneficial to practitioners. Although our studies have revealed an undercurrent of antisocial, hostile, manipulative, and selfish actions, feelings, and motives, the peek into this hidden realm is also reassuring. Informants see that others are having experiences, motives, thoughts, and feelings much like their own. Recognizing the similarities of all beings and the compassion that this facilitates are major themes of Buddhism (Dalai Lama, 1998).

Virtually all major spiritual and self-development disciplines cultivate some form of self-observation, and for several of them, it is a primary and essential feature of their practice. Buddhism, Yoga, Taoism, contemplative Christianity and Judaism, Islamic mysticism, Western psychotherapy, and a number of other disciplines urge "turning inward." The practice of self-observation and its cousin, meditation, are seen as the primary avenues to personal and spiritual growth. Self-observation practices are used by the spiritual, religious, and therapeutic traditions to promote peace, happiness, balance, patience, compassion, altruism, heightened awareness, and love (Beck, 1989; Dalai Lama, 1998; Hanh, 1987; James, 1929; Kornfield, 1993; Moore, 1992; Ramacharaka, 1906; Underhill, 1911; Vilayat, 1974).

The Eastern spiritual traditions of Buddhism and Yoga turn toward meditation, reflexivity, and mindfulness in daily life. In his book *The Miracle of Mindfulness: A Manual on Meditation* (1987), Thich Nhat Hanh wrote, "You've got to practice meditation when you are . . . sweeping the floor, drinking tea, talking to friends, or whatever you are doing" (pp. 23-24). To a small degree, the SSO instructions also ask the informant to be mindful (at least aware enough) at all times to capture the moment when the targeted phenomenon pops up.

Moreover, SSO follows the same concern as Buddhist and psychotherapeutic practices: to observe calmly and accurately, without analyzing or judging. In her book *Everyday Zen*, Beck (1989) described a meditation practice that is a variant of SSO. She told meditators to observe their stream of consciousness and to *label* the contents. She wrote:

> Be specific in your labeling: not just "thinking, thinking" or "worrying, worrying," but a specific label. For example: "Having a thought she's very bossy." "Having a thought that he's very unfair to me." "Having a thought that I never

do anything right." Be specific. . . . When we label thoughts precisely and carefully, what happens to them? They begin to quiet down . . . and as we do it our life transforms. (pp. 26-27)

What is going on in the various practices of religious reflexivity and attentive self-observing? What happens when an individual engages in the Buddhist practice of mindfully observing? George Herbert Mead's (1956) famous distinction between the "I" and the "me" identifies a duality of the self. On the one side is the spontaneous, unpredictable, and always elusive observer, the essential subject, the "I"—and on the other is the social self, the object of self-scrutiny—the role-playing "me."

The observing self may be what spiritual traditions describe as "the eye of the eye and the ear of the ear," meaning that "the watcher" who is receiving the data from the senses is the somewhat mysterious and atemporal "I." Is the receiving subject to whom all information is the object of observation the gateway to what religious traditions identify as the spiritual quality of the psyche? If so, then maybe, to whatever small degree, the reflexive work of practicing SSO brings the informants a little closer to their Center.

NOTES

1. Compared with studies employing a positivistic paradigm, qualitative studies tend to reverse the concern for making type 1 and type 2 errors. Qualitative researchers are anxious not to miss an organizational pattern that may yield an insight (Schwartz & Jacobs, 1979).

2. Some social scientists have developed accurate descriptions and insightful analyses and understandings of everyday life by using the self-observation experiences and data drawn from a single informant. If the phenomenon being studied is universal, then even just one informant can yield valid data. The viability of the sample-of-one approach is demonstrated by the linguist who can build a descriptive analysis of a language using one representative competent speaker (e.g., Whorf, 1956). In the final analysis, the universality and representativeness of the data need to be empirically demonstrated.

3. The Japanese call the form of lying described *tattemai*.

4. One ingenious informant carried a tape recorder with her. As soon as it was practically possible, she reconstructed the observation by speaking into the tape recorder and later transcribing the taped description into written field notes. The speed and immediacy of using an audio tape recorder is likely to improve the quality of the SSO data.

5. This study was coauthored with Joseph Tracewell.

REFERENCES

Atkinson, J. M., & Heritage, J. (1984). *Structures of social action: Studies in conversation analysis.* Cambridge, UK: Cambridge University Press.

Beck, C. J. (1989). *Everyday Zen.* San Francisco: HarperCollins.

Bellman, B. (1984). *The language of secrecy: Symbols and metaphors in Poro ritual.* New Brunswick, NJ: Rutgers University Press.

Bergmann, J. (1993). *Discreet indiscretions: The social organization of gossip.* New York: Aldine De Gruyter.

Brown, P., & Levinson, S. (1987). *Politeness: Some universals in language usage.* Cambridge, UK: Cambridge University Press.

Caughey, J. L. (1982). Ethnography, introspection, and reflexive cultural studies. In J. Salzman (Ed.), *Prospects: The Annual of American Cultural Studies, 7,* 115-139.

Caughey, J. L. (1984). *Imaginary social worlds: A cultural approach.* Lincoln: University of Nebraska Press.

Cicourel, A. (1964). *Method and measurement in sociology.* Glencoe, IL: Free Press.

Clark, C. (1987). Sympathy biography and sympathy margin. *American Journal of Sociology, 93,* 290-321.

Cooley, C. H. (1926). The roots of social knowledge. *American Journal of Sociology, 32,* 59-79.

Crapanzano, V. (1970). The writing of ethnography. *Dialectical Anthropology, 2,* 69-73.

Dalai Lama. (1998). *The art of happiness.* New York: Simon & Schuster.

Denzin, N. (1971). The logic of naturalistic inquiry. *Social Forces, 50,* 166-182.

Dilthey, W. (1976). *Selected writings* (H. P. Hickman, Ed. & Trans.). Cambridge, UK: Cambridge University Press.

Duck, S. W. (1991). Diaries and logs. In B. M. Montgomery & S. W. Duck (Eds.), *Studying social interaction* (pp. 141-161). New York: Guilford.

Duck, S. W., & Rutt, D. (1988, February). *The experience of everyday relational conversations: Are all communications created equal?* Paper presented at the annual convention of the Speech Communication Association, New Orleans, LA.

Ellis, C. (1991). Sociological introspection and emotional experience. *Symbolic Interaction, 14,* 23-50.

Festinger, L. (1954). A theory of social comparison. *Human Relations, 7,* 114-140.

Garfinkel, H. (1967). *Studies in ethnomethodology.* Englewood Cliffs, NJ: Prentice Hall.

Garfinkel, H., & Sacks, H. (1970). On formal structures of practical actions. In J. C. McKinney & E. A. Tirayakian (Eds.), *Theoretical sociology* (pp. 338-366). New York: Appleton-Century-Crofts.

Genest, M., & Turk, D. C. (1981). Think-aloud approaches to cognitive assessment. In T. V. Merluzzi, C. R. Glass, & M. Genest (Eds.), *Cognitive assessment.* New York: Guilford.

63

Glowacz, C. (1989). *Secrets within secrets: The untold stories.* Unpublished student paper, California State University, Dominguez Hills.

Goffman, E. (1959). *The presentation of self in everyday life.* New York: Doubleday.

Goffman, E. (1967). *Interaction ritual: Essays in face-to-face behavior.* Chicago: Aldine.

Goodwin, C., & Goodwin, M. (1990). Interstitial arguments. In A. Grimshaw (Ed.), *Conflict talk* (pp. 85-117). Cambridge, UK: Cambridge University Press.

Goodwin, M. (1982). Processes of dispute management among urban black children. *American Ethnologist, 9,* 76-96.

Goodwin, M. (1983). Aggravated correction and disagreement in children's conversations. *Journal of Pragmatics, 7,* 657-677.

Grover, S. (1982). A re-evaluation of the introspection controversy: Additional considerations. *Journal of General Psychology, 106,* 202-212.

Gubrium, J., & Holstein, J. (1997). *The new language of qualitative method.* New York: Oxford University Press.

Hanh, T. N. (1987). *The miracle of mindfulness: A manual on meditation* (Rev. ed.). Boston: Beacon.

Harre, R. (1986). An outline of the social constructionist viewpoint. In R. Harre (Ed.), *The social construction of emotions.* New York: Basil Blackwell.

Hayano, D. M. (1979). Auto-ethnography: Paradigms, problems and prospects. *Human Organization, 38,* 99-104.

Heritage, J. (1984). *Garfinkel and ethnomethodology.* Cambridge, UK: Polity.

Hinkle, R., & Hinkle, G. (1954). *The development of modern sociology: Its nature and growth in the United States.* New York: Random House.

Hochschild, A. (1983). *The managed heart.* Berkeley: University of California Press.

Holtgraves, T. (1992). Linguistic realization of face management: Implications for language production and comprehension, person perception and cross-cultural communication. *Social Psychology Quarterly, 55,* 141-159.

James, W. (1929). *The varieties of religious experience.* New York: Random House.

Johnson, J. (1975). *Doing field research.* New York: Free Press.

Jung, C. G. (1961). *Memories, dreams, reflections.* New York: Random House.

Katz, J. (1999). *How emotions work.* Chicago: University of Chicago Press.

Kirk, J., & Miller, M. (1986). *Reliability and validity in qualitative research.* Beverly Hills, CA: Sage.

Kornfield, J. (1993). *A path with heart.* New York: Bantam.

Krieger, S. (1985). Beyond subjectivity: The use of self in social science. *Qualitative Sociology, 8,* 309-324.

Markus, H., & Zajonc, R. B. (1985). The cognitive perspectives in social psychology. In G. Lindzey & E. Aronson (Eds.), *Handbook of social psychology* (3rd ed., Vol. 1, pp. 137-230). New York: Random House.

Maynard, D. (1985). How children start arguments. *Language and Society, 14,* 1-29.

Mead, G. H. (1956). *George Herbert Mead on social psychology: Selected papers* (A. Strauss, Ed.). Chicago: University of Chicago Press.

Moore, T. (1992). *The care of the soul.* New York: Harper Perennial.

Nickerson, R. S., & Adams, M. J. (1979). Long-term memory for a common object. *Cognitive Psychology, 11,* 287-307.

Pence, A., & Paymar, M. (1986). *Power and control: Tactics of men who batter.* Minneapolis: Minnesota Program Development.

Polanyi, M. (1967). *The tacit dimension.* New York: Anchor.

64

Pomerantz, A. (1978). Compliment responses: Notes on the co-operation of multiple constraints. In J. Schenkein (Ed.), *Studies in the organization of conversational interaction* (pp. 79-112). New York: Academic Press.

Progoff, I. (1975). *At a journal workshop.* New York: Dialogue House Library.

Psathas, G. (1995). *Conversation analysis: The study of talk-in-interaction.* Thousand Oaks, CA: Sage.

Ramacharaka, Y. (1906). *Raja yoga or mental development.* Chicago: Yoga Publication Society.

Reis, H. T., & Wheeler, L. (1991). Studying social interaction with the Rochester Interaction Record. New York: Academic Press.

Rodriguez, N., & Ryave, A. L. (1990). Telling lies in everyday life: Motivational and organizational consequences of sequential preferences. *Qualitative Sociology, 13,* 195-210.

Rodriguez, N., & Ryave, A. L. (1992). The structural organization and micropolitics of everyday secret telling interactions. *Qualitative Sociology, 15,* 297-318.

Rodriguez, N., & Ryave, A. L. (1993, March). *On the non-verbalization of self-other comparisons in everyday life.* Paper presented at the annual meeting of the Pacific Sociological Association, Portland, OR.

Rodriguez, N., & Ryave, A. L. (1995). The competitive management of face: A case study of mentally retarded adult male interaction. *Semiotica, 103,* 97-117.

Rodriguez, N., & Ryave, A. L. (1998, March). *The process of social comparison and the engendering of envy in everyday life.* Paper presented at the annual meeting of the Pacific Sociological Association, San Francisco.

Rodriguez, N., Ryave, A. L., & Tracewell, J. (1998). Withholding compliments in everyday life and the covert management of disaffiliation. *Journal of Contemporary Ethnography, 27,* 323-345.

Rogers, C. R. (1961). *On becoming a person: A therapist's view of psychotherapy.* Boston: Houghton Mifflin.

Rose, S. D., & LeCroy, C. W. (1991). Group methods. In F. H. Kanfer & A. P. Goldstein (Eds.), *Helping people change* (4th ed., pp. 422-453). Elmsford, NY: Pergamon.

Rosenberg, M. (1979). *Conceiving the self.* New York: Basic Books.

Sabini, J., & Silver, M. (1982). *Moralities of everyday life.* Oxford, UK: Oxford University Press.

Sacks, H. (1963). Sociological description. *Berkeley Journal of Sociology, 8,* 1-17.

Sacks, H. (1970a). *Winter Lecture 2.* Unpublished lecture, University of California, Irvine.

Sacks, H. (1970b). *Spring Lecture 1.* Unpublished lecture, University of California, Irvine.

Sacks, H. (1975). Everyone has to lie. In J. Sanchez & M. Blount (Eds.), *Sociocultural dimensions of language use* (pp. 57-80). New York: Academic Press.

Sacks, H. (1987). On preferences for agreement and continuity in sequences in conversation. In G. Button & J. Lee (Eds.), *Talk and social organization* (pp. 54-69). Clevedon, UK: Multilingual Matters.

Sacks, H. (1992). Lecture 29. In G. Jefferson (Ed.), *Lectures on conversation* (pp. 461-466). Oxford, UK: Basil Blackwell.

Salovey, P. (1991). Social comparison processes in envy and jealousy. In J. Suls & T. Wills (Eds.), *Social comparison: Contemporary theory and research* (pp. 261-285). Hillsdale, NJ: Lawrence Erlbaum.

Schegloff, E. (1980). Preliminaries to preliminaries: "Can I ask a question?" *Sociological Inquiry, 50,* 104-152.

Schegloff, E., Jefferson, G., & Sacks, H. (1977). The preference for self-correction in the organization of repair in conversation. *Language, 53,* 361-382.

Schegloff, E., & Sacks, H. (1973). Opening up closings. *Semiotica, 8,* 289-327.

Schneider, W., & Shiffrin, R. M. (1977). Controlled and automatic human information processing: I. Detection, search, and attention. *Psychological Review, 84,* 1-66.

Schoeck, H. (1969). *Envy: A theory of social behavior.* New York: Harcourt, Brace & World.

Schutz, A. (1962). *The collected papers I: The problem of social reality* (M. Natanson, Ed.). The Hague: Martinus Nijhoff.

Schwartz, H., & Jacobs, J. (1979). *Qualitative sociology: A method to the madness.* New York: Free Press.

Silverman, D. (1993). *Interpreting qualitative data: Methods for analyzing talk, text and interaction.* Newbury Park, CA: Sage.

Simmel, G. (1950). *The sociology of George Simmel* (K. Wolf, Trans.). New York: Macmillan.

Singer, J. L. (1966). *Daydreaming: An introduction to the experimental study of inner experience.* New York: Random House.

Singer, J. L. (1975). *Inner world of daydreaming.* New York: Harper & Row.

Sudnow, D. (1978). *The ways of the hand.* Cambridge, MA: Harvard University Press.

Suls, J. & Wills, T. (1991). *Social comparison: Contemporary theory and research.* Hillsdale, NJ: Lawrence Erlbaum.

Tessar, A. (1991). Emotion in social comparison and reflection processes. In J. Suls & T. Wills (Eds.), *Social comparison: Contemporary theory and research* (pp. 115-145). Hillsdale, NJ: Lawrence Erlbaum.

Underhill, E. (1911). *Mysticism.* New York: Dutton.

Vilayat, P. (1974). *Toward the one.* New York: Harper & Row.

Wallace, A. F. (1972). Driving to work. In J. P. Spradley (Ed.), *Culture and cognition* (pp. 311-329). San Francisco: Chandler.

Watson, J. B. (1913). Psychology as the behaviorist views it. *Psychological Review, 20,* 158-177.

Weber, M. (1949). *The methodology of the social sciences* (E. Shils & H. Finch, Eds.). Glencoe, IL: Free Press.

Weber, M. (1967). *Max Weber on law and economy in society* (M. Reinstein, Ed.). New York: Simon & Schuster.

Wheeler, L., & Nezlek, J. (1977). Sex differences in social participation. *Journal of Personality and Social Psychology, 35,* 742-754.

Wheeler, L., & Reis, H. T. (1991). Self-recording of everyday life events: Origins, types and uses. *Journal of Personality, 59,* 340-353.

Wheeler, L., Reis, H. T., & Nezlek, J. (1983). Loneliness, social interaction and sex roles. *Journal of Personality and Social Psychology, 45,* 943-953.

Whorf, B. (1956). *Language, thought and reality: Selected writings.* Cambridge: MIT Press.

Wieder, D. L., & Zimmerman, D. (1977). The diary: Diary-interview method. *Urban Life, 5,* 479-498.

Wolfson, N., & Manes, J. (1980). The compliment as a social strategy. *Papers in Linguistics, 13,* 391-410.

Wong, M. M., & Csikszentmihalyi, M. (1991). Motivation and academic achievement: The effects of personality traits and the quality of experience. *Journal of Personality, 59,* 539-574.

Wood, J. V. (1989). Theory and research concerning social comparisons of personal attributes. *Psychological Bulletin, 106,* 231-248.

Zautra, A. J., Finch, J. F., Reich, J. W., & Guarnaccia, C. A. (1991). Predicting the everyday life events of older adults. *Journal of Personality, 59,* 507-538.

Znaniecki, F. (1934). *The method of sociology.* New York: Farrar & Rinehart.

ABOUT THE AUTHORS

As coauthors, Noelie Rodriguez and Alan L. Ryave acknowledge each other as equals in the preparation of their work.

Dr. Noelie Rodriguez is Associate Professor of Sociology at Hawaii Community College. She received a BA in sociology and English at the University of South Florida and an MA and PhD at the University of California, Los Angeles, in sociology. She has a background of work in quantitative methods, social problems, theory, stratification, the sociology of knowledge, and several other areas. She engages in social issues activism. Her writings on political economy, criminology, and women's studies have been published in *Gender and Society, Capitalism, Nature, Socialism*, the *Prison Journal*, and the *Journal of Applied Behavioral Science*. Her work in the study of everyday life has appeared in *Qualitative Sociology, Shakaigakku Ronso, Semiotica*, and the *Journal of Contemporary Ethnography*.

Dr. Alan L. Ryave is Professor of Sociology at California State University at Dominguez Hills. He received his BA, MA, and PhD in sociology at the University of California, Los Angeles. Some of his research in the study of everyday life has been published in *Qualitative Sociology, Shakaigakku Ronso, Semiotica*, the *Journal of Contemporary Ethnography, Studies in the Organization of Conversational Interaction*, and *Ethnomethodology*.

Qualitative Research Methods

Series Editor
JOHN VAN MAANEN
Massachusetts Institute of Technology

Associate Editors:
Peter K. Manning, *Michigan State University*
& Marc L. Miller, *University of Washington*

Other volumes in this series listed on outside back cover